CHAPMAN

Text
DENIS BERNARD
Drawings and colour
NEDZAD KAMENICA
CHRISTIAN PAPAZOGLAKIS
ROBERT PAQUET
TANJA CINNA
Translation
KEN SMITH

This book was first published in France by Editions Glénat in three volumes as follows:
Volume 1: *Chapman: Les Premières Victoires* (2012)
Volume 2: *Chapman: Les Années Sang et Or* (2012)
Volume 3: *Chapman: Splendeur et Drames* (2013)

This English-language edition first published by Haynes Publishing in September 2013

A catalogue record for this book is available from the British Library

ISBN 978 0 85733 471 8

Library of Congress catalog card no. 2013941309

Haynes Publishing, Sparkford, Yeovil, Somerset BA22 7JJ, UK
E-mail: sales@haynes.co.uk
Website: www.haynes.co.uk

Printed and bound in the USA by Odcombe Press LP,
1299 Bridgestone Parkway, La Vergne, TN 37086

'Colin Chapman' is a registered trademark of the Estate of ACB Chapman

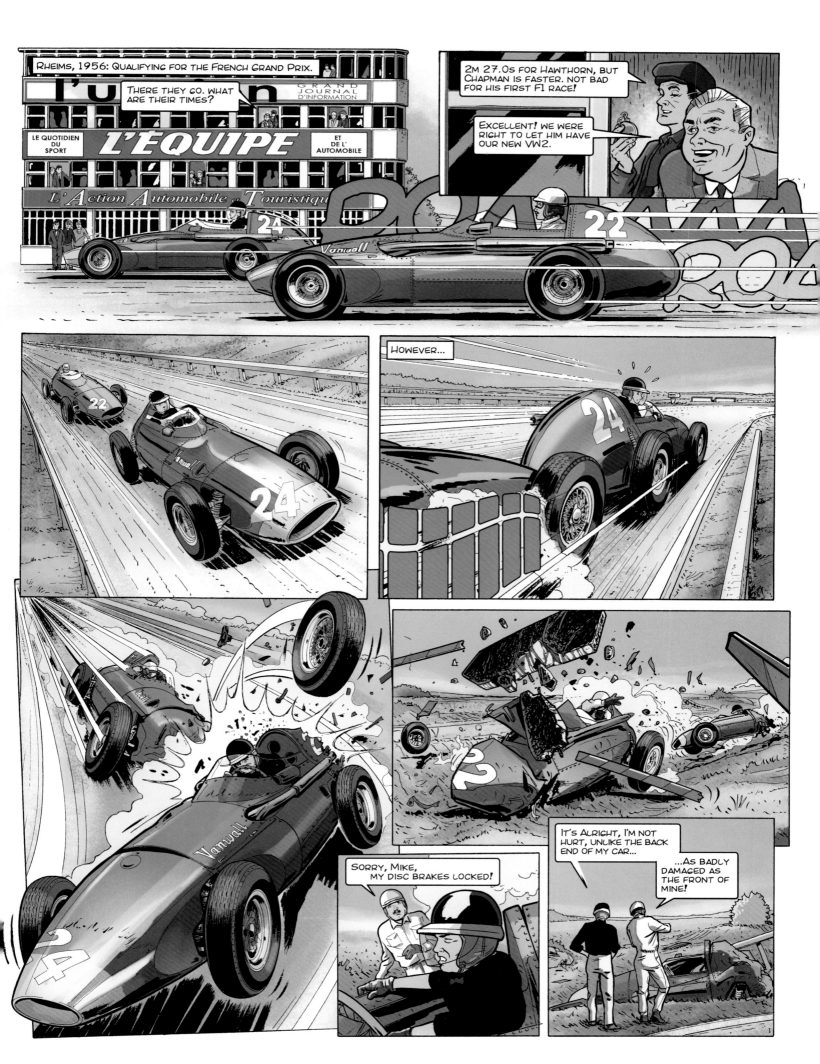

THE MECHANICS HAVE WORKED HARD TO PUT TOGETHER A SINGLE CAR FROM THE WRECKAGE OF TWO. BUT THERE CAN BE ONLY ONE DRIVER...

VANWALL VW2:
VANWALL ENGINE
FOUR CYLINDERS IN LINE,
2,490cc
TWIN OHC, TWO VALVES PER
CYLINDER
260BHP AT 7,500RPM
FIVE-SPEED GEARBOX,
TUBULAR STEEL CHASSIS,
ALUMINIUM BODY
570KG

THOUGH CHAPMAN MANAGED TO COME FIFTH IN QUALIFYING, BETWEEN HIS TWO TEAM-MATES, HARRY SCHELL AND MIKE HAWTHORN, IT WOULD BE HAWTHORN WHO WOULD DRIVE THE REBUILT VANWALL!

COLIN CHAPMAN WAS ALREADY A SUCCESSFUL DRIVER OF HIS OWN-BRAND LOTUS CARS IN F2, BUT HE WOULD NEVER AGAIN GET THE CHANCE TO RACE IN F1.

TONY VANDERVELL, THE BOSS OF VANWALL, ENTRUSTED THE DESIGN OF THE VW2'S CHASSIS TO COLIN CHAPMAN AND THE BODYWORK TO FRANK COSTIN. DURING THE NEXT SEASON, ITS SUCCESSOR, THE VW5, WOULD WIN SEVERAL GRANDS PRIX.

MONACO 1958, AND TEAM LOTUS IS JUST GETTING STARTED IN F1. CHAPMAN HAS DEVELOPED AN F1 CAR FROM THE F2 LOTUS 12.

GRAHAM HILL RETIRES AND BUT CLIFF ALLISON COMES HOME AN EXCELLENT SIXTH, 13 LAPS BEHIND THE WINNER, MAURICE TRINTIGNANT.

LOTUS 12:
CLIMAX FPF ENGINE
FOUR CYLINDERS IN LINE,
1,976cc
TWIN OHC, TWO VALVES
PER CYLINDER
176BHP AT 6,500RPM
FIVE-SPEED GEARBOX,
TUBULAR STEEL CHASSIS
300KG

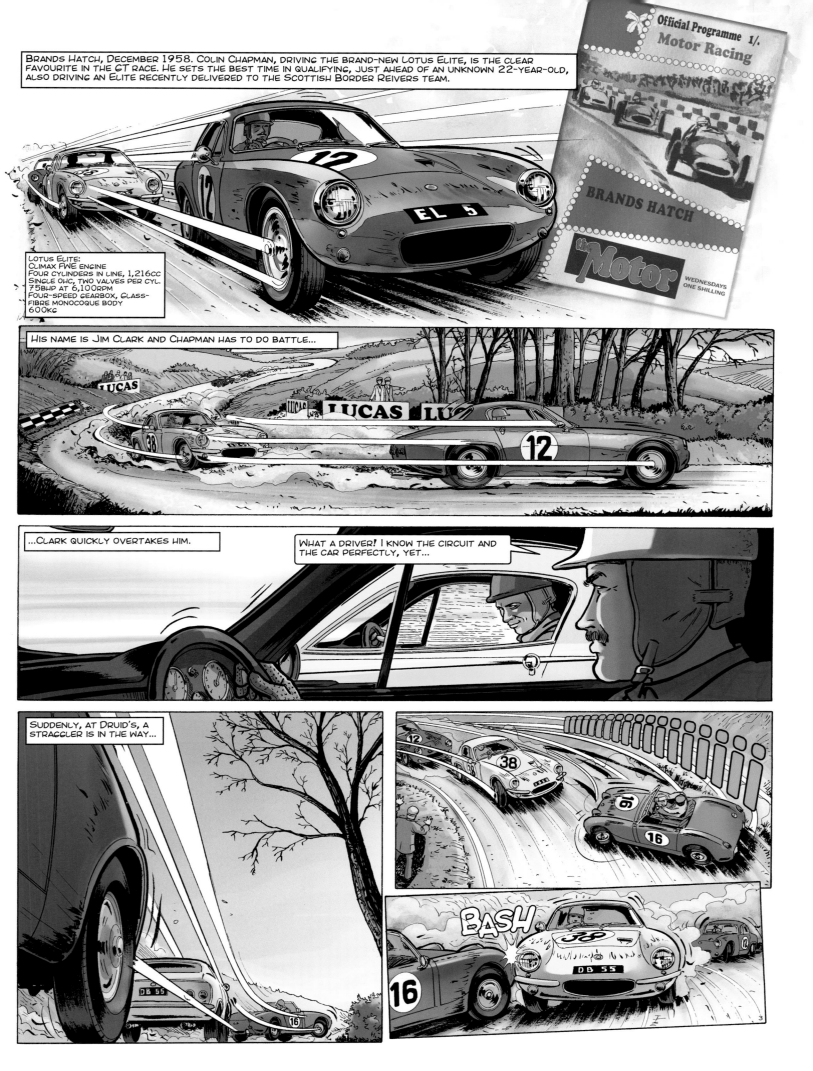

BRANDS HATCH, DECEMBER 1958. COLIN CHAPMAN, DRIVING THE BRAND-NEW LOTUS ELITE, IS THE CLEAR FAVOURITE IN THE GT RACE. HE SETS THE BEST TIME IN QUALIFYING, JUST AHEAD OF AN UNKNOWN 22-YEAR-OLD, ALSO DRIVING AN ELITE RECENTLY DELIVERED TO THE SCOTTISH BORDER REIVERS TEAM.

Official Programme 1/.
Motor Racing

BRANDS HATCH

the Motor
WEDNESDAYS
ONE SHILLING

LOTUS ELITE:
CLIMAX FWE ENGINE
FOUR CYLINDERS IN LINE, 1,216CC
SINGLE OHC, TWO VALVES PER CYL.
75BHP AT 6,100RPM
FOUR-SPEED GEARBOX, GLASS-
FIBRE MONOCOQUE BODY
600KG

HIS NAME IS JIM CLARK AND CHAPMAN HAS TO DO BATTLE...

...CLARK QUICKLY OVERTAKES HIM.

WHAT A DRIVER! I KNOW THE CIRCUIT AND THE CAR PERFECTLY, YET...

SUDDENLY, AT DRUID'S, A STRAGGLER IS IN THE WAY...

BASH

5

IF THAT HADN'T HAPPENED, HE WOULD HAVE GIVEN ME QUITE A LESSON...

YOU SHOULD HAVE SEEN IT, HAZEL, THAT JIM CLARK'S A KID WHO'S COME FROM NOWHERE – AN AMAZING TALENT!

HE WAS ALL OVER ME IN THAT RACE. AND WITH ONE OF MY OWN CARS INTO THE BARGAIN!

MAYBE IT'S TIME FOR ME TO GIVE UP DRIVING.

DESIGNING AND DEVELOPING NEW MODELS, ORGANISING PRODUCTION, MEETING CUSTOMERS, MANAGING TEAM LOTUS...

I THINK THAT'S WHAT SUITS ME BEST...

I WANT TO GIVE MYSELF THE MEANS FOR TEAM LOTUS TO GET TO THE VERY TOP ONE DAY.

I'M SURE YOU'LL MAKE IT, COLIN.

WE WILL MAKE IT!

4

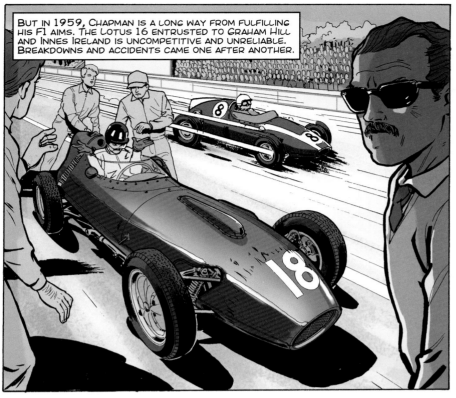

BUT IN 1959, CHAPMAN IS A LONG WAY FROM FULFILLING HIS F1 AIMS. THE LOTUS 16 ENTRUSTED TO GRAHAM HILL AND INNES IRELAND IS UNCOMPETITIVE AND UNRELIABLE. BREAKDOWNS AND ACCIDENTS CAME ONE AFTER ANOTHER.

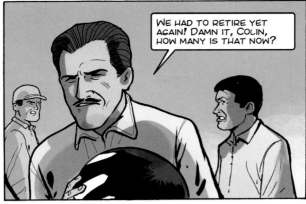

WE HAD TO RETIRE YET AGAIN! DAMN IT, COLIN, HOW MANY IS THAT NOW?

AND WHERE HAS INNES GOT TO?

HE LOOKS PRETTY BUSY, AS USUAL!

GRAHAM! THE TEAM'S ALL HERE, LET'S HAVE A PARTY!

LOTUS FINISHES THE SEASON LAST IN THE CONSTRUCTORS' CHAMPIONSHIP, A LONG WAY BEHIND COOPER-CLIMAX, FERRARI AND BRM.

NEAR THE END OF THE SEASON...

SORRY, COLIN! BRM HAVE OFFERED ME A GOOD CONTRACT FOR NEXT SEASON. I'M LEAVING LOTUS!

WHAT?

BUT GRAHAM, YOU CAN'T DO THAT TO ME, NOT AFTER ALL I'VE DONE FOR YOU!!

COLIN, YOUR CARS AREN'T ROBUST ENOUGH! YOU KNOW WHAT EVERYONE IS TELLING ME AFTER THESE ENDLESS MECHANICAL FAILURES?

"DON'T STAY AT LOTUS, YOU'LL END UP GETTING KILLED!"

MY CARS ARE DESIGNED TO BE LIGHT AND POWERFUL! WHEN A PART BREAKS, WE STRENGTHEN IT, BUT I REFUSE TO ADD WEIGHT TO MY CARS NEEDLESSLY!

LET'S BE HONEST, THE PAST TWO SEASONS HAVE BEEN A DISASTER.

AND WITHOUT ME, YOU'D STILL BE GETTING YOUR HANDS DIRTY WORKING ON MY CARS RATHER THAN DRIVING THEM. DON'T FORGET THAT!

5

AND DON'T BOTHER COMING TO WATKINS GLEN! I DON'T EVER WANT TO SEE YOU ON MY PREMISES AGAIN.

IS THAT CLEAR?!

FINE!

GÉRARD CROMBAC, COLIN CHAPMAN'S RIGHT-HAND MAN, JOINS HIM.

TRAITOR!

WHAT ON EARTH'S GOING ON, COLIN?

OH, JABBY, GRAHAM IS LEAVING US. THAT'S WHAT'S GOING ON! AS IF THE SITUATION WASN'T BAD ENOUGH AS IT IS!

A LAD JOINED US AS A MECHANIC AND I TURNED HIM INTO A FORMULA 1 DRIVER! AND NOW HE'S OFF TO JOIN THE OPPOSITION...

BUT YOU'VE STILL GOT INNES!

IRELAND'S A VERY GOOD DRIVER, TOO, BUT HE PREFERS PARTYING TO WORKING ON DEVELOPMENT...

HILL DOES TEN TIMES AS MUCH WORK AS HE DOES.

WELL, YES, HE'S A VERY FAST AND HARD-WORKING DRIVER, BUT CERTAINLY NOT IRREPLACEABLE. THERE'S REALLY NO NEED TO GET IN SUCH A STATE ABOUT IT, COLIN!

YOU'RE RIGHT, I GET CARRIED AWAY SO EASILY.

COME OUTSIDE WITH ME, COLIN. I'VE BEEN LENT A NEW JAGUAR XK150. WHY DON'T WE TAKE IT FOR A SPIN?

THANK GOODNESS I CAN RELY ON YOUR FRIENDSHIP, JABBY!

6

IN HORNSEY, NORTH LONDON, SIX YEARS EARLIER.

HURRY UP AND FINISH TIDYING UP, HE SHOULD BE HERE IN A FEW MINUTES!

EXCUSE ME, I'M LOOKING FOR MR CHAPMAN, COLIN CHAPMAN.

YES, THAT'S ME.

GREAT TO MEET YOU, I'M GÉRARD CROMBAC.

DELIGHTED... DO COME IN!

HOW OLD IS HE – 15? CAN HE REALLY BE A COLUMNIST ON A RESPECTED MAGAZINE LIKE AUTOSPORT?

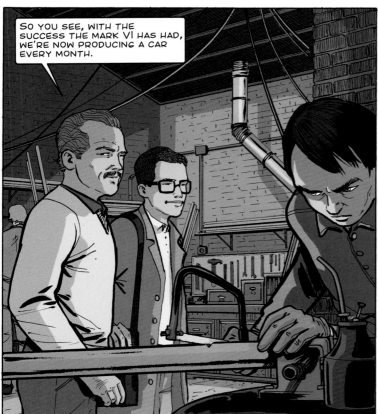

SO YOU SEE, WITH THE SUCCESS THE MARK VI HAS HAD, WE'RE NOW PRODUCING A CAR EVERY MONTH.

MR CHAPMAN, WOULD YOU BE PREPARED TO SELL ME THE CAR YOU RACE?

LOTUS MK VI:
FORD ENGINE, FOUR CYLINDERS IN LINE, 1,172CC
TWO VALVES PER CYLINDER
50BHP AT 5,000RPM
THREE-SPEED GEARBOX
TUBULAR STEEL CHASSIS, ALUMINIUM BODYWORK
432KG

You're asking a lot. I'm due to race at Brands Hatch next weekend... I suppose I could let you have it for £450!*

It's more than I was thinking of paying. Still, I want to win races...

OK, agreed. It's a deal!

*EQUIVALENT TO £11,000 NOW

I built the first Lotus, the Mk 1, in 1948, and I set up my company in 1952. Even now I still have a day job, designing bridges for the British Aluminium Company...

...And in the evening I work on the Mark VI.

Sales are improving all the time thanks to the race wins and John Bolster's article in your magazine.

What are your current plans?

Racing at Le Mans and building an F1 car.

When you come to France, get in touch with me. I'd be delighted to help!

Following the 1956 Le Mans 24-hour race, Gérard, now known as 'Jabby', would gradually become right-hand man to Chapman, who valued him for his calmness under pressure and his excellent contacts. The Frenchman, too, would end up abandoning his ambition to be a driver.

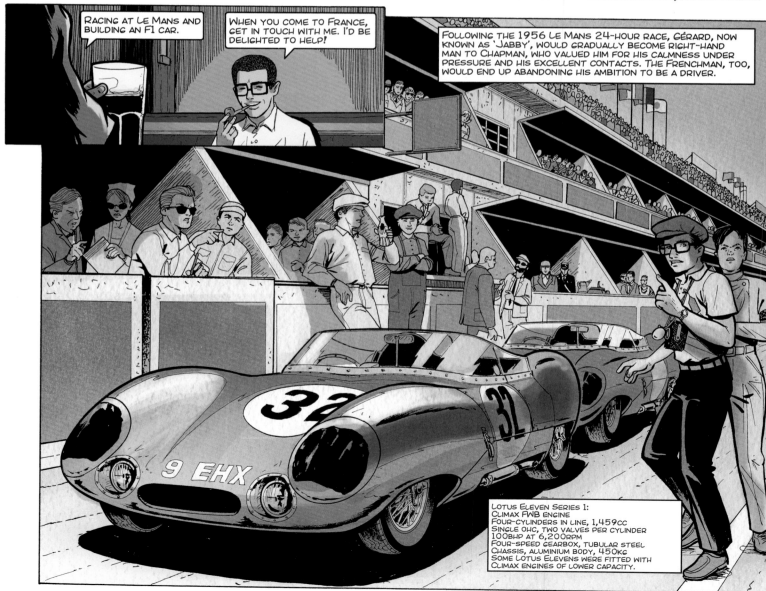

LOTUS ELEVEN SERIES 1:
CLIMAX FWB ENGINE
FOUR-CYLINDERS IN LINE, 1,459CC
SINGLE OHC, TWO VALVES PER CYLINDER
100BHP AT 6,200RPM
FOUR-SPEED GEARBOX, TUBULAR STEEL
CHASSIS, ALUMINIUM BODY, 450KG
SOME LOTUS ELEVENS WERE FITTED WITH
CLIMAX ENGINES OF LOWER CAPACITY.

THE LOTUS FACTORY AT CHESHUNT, NORTH LONDON, 1959.

JABBY, I AM SO ANNOYED WITH MYSELF!

WHY'S THAT?

FOR NOT PUTTING THE ENGINE AT THE REAR. IT CLEARLY GIVES BETTER WEIGHT DISTRIBUTION. COOPER CAME UP WITH IT FIRST... IT SEEMS OBVIOUS IN HINDSIGHT.

AS SOON AS THE COOPER T51 APPEARED, THE WORLD CHAMPIONSHIP WAS PRETTY MUCH DECIDED. QUITE HONESTLY FRONT-ENGINED CARS LOOK LIKE DINOSAURS NOW.

AND BY SELLING HIS CHASSIS TO VARIOUS TEAMS, COOPER HAS TAKEN THE CONSTRUCTORS' TITLE!

COOPER T51:
CLIMAX FPF ENGINE
FOUR CYLINDERS IN LINE, 2,495CC
TWIN OHC, TWO VALVES PER CYL.
240BHP AT 6,750RPM
FOUR-SPEED GEARBOX
TUBULAR STEEL CHASSIS
460KG

WE HAVE TO HAVE AN ANSWER READY FOR NEXT SEASON. LOTUS WILL INTRODUCE A REAR-ENGINED F1 CAR... LOOK.

AN F1 CAR WITH THE 2.5-LITRE CLIMAX ENGINE. IT'LL WEIGH 420KG: 30KG LESS THAN THE COOPER AND 200KG LESS THAN THE FERRARI.

WE'LL BE ABLE TO FIT DIFFERENT ENGINES FOR F2 AND FORMULA JUNIOR RACES AS WELL AS SELLING THE CHASSIS TO LOTS OF TEAMS.

LOTUS 18 JUNIOR:
FORD COSWORTH 105E ENGINE
FOUR CYLINDERS IN LINE, 997CC
OVERHEAD VALVES,
TWO PER CYLINDER
85BHP AT 7,500RPM
FOUR-SPEED GEARBOX
TUBULAR STEEL CHASSIS
GLASS-FIBRE BODY
400KG

GOODWOOD, 1960. CHAPMAN HAS HIRED CLARK, REMEMBERING HIS PERFORMANCE AT BRANDS HATCH! JIM WILL DRIVE THE LOTUS 18 ON ITS DEBUT IN FORMULA JUNIOR.

THIS ISN'T JUST ABOUT RACING AS A SPORT. IF WE CAN BEAT THE COOPERS, LOTUS WILL BE RECOGNISED AS THE BEST IN ITS CLASS AND WE'LL BE ABLE TO SELL OUR CHASSIS TO EVERYONE.

NEWS OF THE WORLD
sponsor the
GT RACE
AND THE B.A.R.C.
FORMULA JUNIOR CHAMPIONSHIP
SAT., 19th MARCH 1960
start 12 noon=finish 6p.m.
2/-
OFFICIAL PROGRAMME
GOODWOOD
RACE ORGANISED BY
BRITISH AUTOMOBILE RACING CLUB

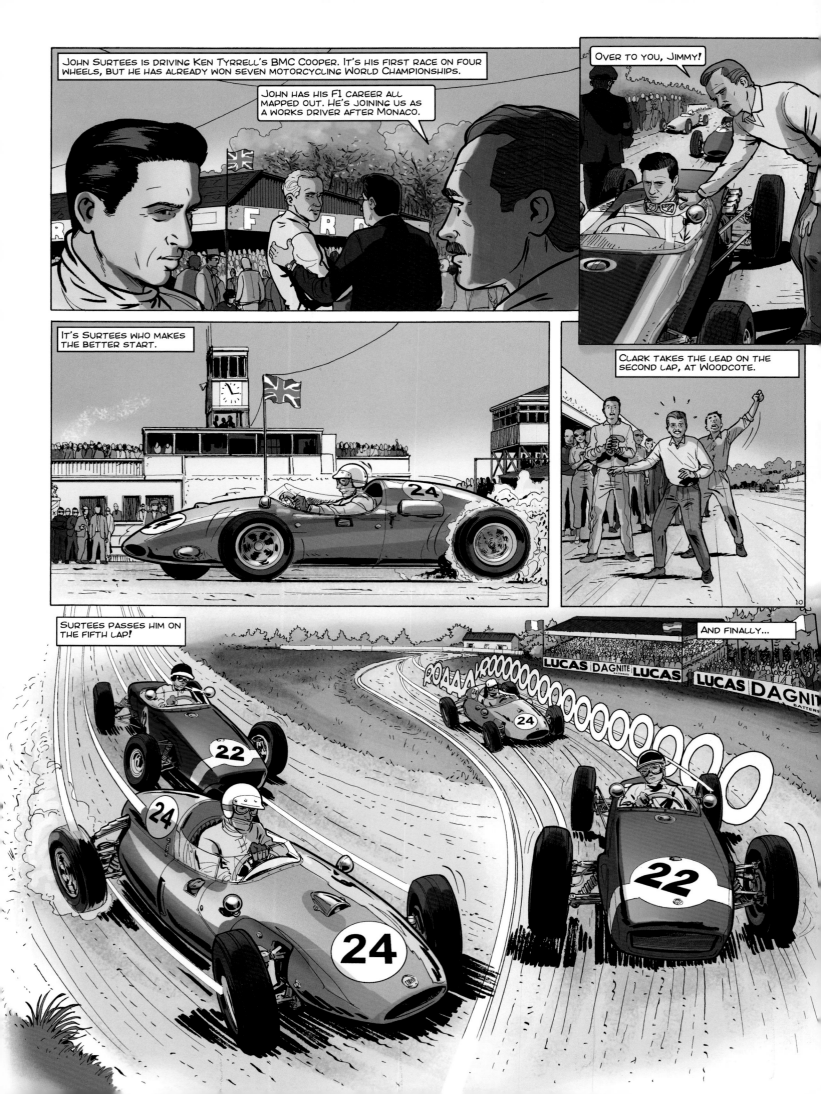

THE LOTUS BEATS THE COOPER AND UNDERLINES THE POINT BY TAKING THE LAP RECORD.

JIM CLARK WOULD GET INTO HIS STRIDE WITH A SEQUENCE OF NINE WINS WITH THE LOTUS IN FORMULA JUNIOR. AND NO FEWER THAN 125 CARS WOULD BE BUILT!

MONACO 1960. JOHN SURTEES, INNES IRELAND AND ALAN STACEY MAKE UP THE WORKS LOTUS TEAM. A FOURTH LOTUS IS ENTERED BY ROB WALKER FOR STIRLING MOSS.

CHAPIONNAT DU MONDE DES ...
XVIIIᵉ GRAND PRIX

MONACO ... MAI 1960

AFTER A THREE-HOUR RACE, STIRLING MOSS BRINGS TEAM LOTUS ITS FIRST F1 WIN AND 'GOD SAVE THE QUEEN' STRIKES UP IN THE PRINCIPALITY.

HEY, COLIN, I'VE SEEN YOU LOOK HAPPIER!?

EVEN THOUGH ROB WALKER IS A FRIEND AND A GOOD CUSTOMER, I ALWAYS PREFER TO SEE MY DRIVERS IN FRONT!

IRELAND FINISHED LAST AND STACEY AND SURTEES HAD TO RETIRE...

JOHN WON'T BE IN HOLLAND. I'VE LET HIM ENTER A MOTORCYCLE RACE. WHO'S GOING TO REPLACE HIM?

WHY NOT JIM CLARK? HE BEAT SURTEES AT GOODWOOD!

11

THE DUTCH GRAND PRIX AND CLARK MAKES HIS F1 DEBUT. HE IS 11TH IN QUALIFYING, SOME WAY BEHIND HIS TWO TEAM-MATES, IRELAND AND STACEY.

LOTUS 18: COVENTRY CLIMAX FPF ENGINE, FOUR CYLINDERS IN LINE, 2,495CC, TWO VALVES PER CYLINDER, TWIN OHC, 240BHP AT 6,750RPM FIVE-SPEED GEARBOX, TUBULAR STEEL CHASSIS, 420KG

THE HOT FAVOURITE IS MOSS, HAVING GOT POLE POSITION WITH THE LOTUS RUN BY ROB WALKER, THE HEIR TO THE SCOTCH WHISKY BRAND.

DURING THE RACE, CLARK WORKS HIS WAY UP TO FIFTH PLACE AND BATTLES RELENTLESSLY WITH GRAHAM HILL IN HIS BRM.

BUT CLARK SUFFERS A MECHANICAL FAILURE.

KRR KRR

SORRY... IT'S THE TRANSMISSION. COULDN'T CHANGE GEAR.

IT'S A FANTASTIC FIRST TRY, A REAL PERFORMANCE! WHAT A DAY!

BRAVO JIMMY!

MOSS WINS AGAIN, AND IRELAND IS SECOND.

...AND HILL GETS HIS FIRST PODIUM PLACE.

NOT SO EASY CATCHING UP WITH A LOTUS WHILE TRYING TO AVOID ALL THE BITS FALLING OFF IT!

EH, COLIN?

JUNE 1960. THE BELGIAN GRAND PRIX AT SPA-FRANCORCHAMPS.

VISITE MEDICALE PILOTES

HEY, JIMMY, OVER HERE. YOU NEED TO HAVE YOUR MEDICAL CHECK-UP!

THANKS, INNES... I'VE JUST HAD IT.

NO, COME ON. WE NEED A FEW PEOPLE AROUND ALAN FOR THIS TO WORK.

?!

NEXT... TAKE A SEAT. YOUR NAME?

STACEY... ALAN... TEAM LOTUS.

REFLEXES... VERY GOOD.

NOW THE OTHER LEG.

OK DOCTOR.

DOCTOR !!

IT REALLY HURTS WHEN I SIT DOWN, DOCTOR, HELP ME!

WHAT ON EARTH...

STOP PLAYING THE FOOL, WILL YOU?

ESS, GOCTOR.

THAT'S THE SAME LEG, ISN'T IT?

SHHH!

PERFECT.

BUT DURING PRACTICE...

HE WOULD HAVE HAD A JOB TESTING THE OTHER ONE... I LOST IT 10 YEARS AGO IN A MOTORCYCLE ACCIDENT! THANKS TO INNES, IT ALWAYS WORKS!

ALAN HAS HAD A MOTORCYCLE TWISTGRIP FITTED TO HIS CAR.

13

IRELAND STOPS IN
THE PITS.

IT'S STIRLING MOSS. HE
CAME OFF AT BURNENVILLE.

HE LOST A REAR
WHEEL AT OVER
120MPH!

MIKE, LEND ME YOUR HELMET
AND YOUR CAR. I'VE GOT TO
GO AND SEE HIM!

MOSS HAS BROKEN HIS NOSE, BOTH LEGS
AND HAS SEVERAL CRACKED VERTEBRAE.

LATER IN PRACTICE, MIKE TAYLOR,
ALSO IN A LOTUS...

CRAK!

AFTER HIS STEERING COLUMN
BREAKS, TAYLOR IS THROWN
OUT, SUSTAINING MULTIPLE
FRACTURES.

IT'S THE END OF HIS
RACING CAREER.

WITH PRACTICE OVER, THE
ATMOSPHERE IS ESPECIALLY GLOOMY.

14

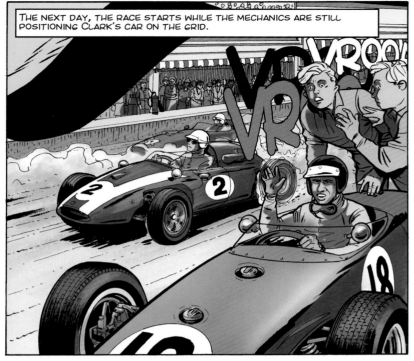

THE NEXT DAY, THE RACE STARTS WHILE THE MECHANICS ARE STILL POSITIONING CLARK'S CAR ON THE GRID.

VROOM

AFTER A FEW LAPS, THE YOUNG CHRIS BRISTOW IS BATTLING IT OUT WITH THE LOCAL HERO, WILLY MAIRESSE, IN A FERRARI. THEY ARE WHEEL-TO-WHEEL AT BURNENVILLE. BRISTOW IS PUSHED OUT WIDE, OFF THE RACING LINE.

OH MY GOD, WHO IS IT THIS TIME?!

CHRIS... POOR CHAP. IT'S AWFUL.

15

ALAN STACEY CAREERS OFF THE TRACK AFTER BEING HIT IN THE FACE BY A BIRD AT OVER 150MPH. HIS CAR ENDS UP IN A FIELD AND CATCHES FIRE.

HE'S KILLED ON THE SPOT.

OF THE FIVE LOTUSES ENTERED, ONLY CLARK'S CROSSES THE FINISHING LINE, IN A VERY RESPECTABLE FIFTH PLACE.

IT'S HORRIBLE!

OH MY GOD!

IF THAT'S RACING... I'M UTTERLY SICKENED.

I'D RATHER GIVE UP!

WE'VE ALL BEEN SHOCKED AT WHAT HAPPENED AT SPA THE OTHER DAY, YOU PROBABLY MORE THAN MOST!

AND YET...

IF WE SUCCEED IN PUTTING OUR FEELINGS ASIDE, WE CAN GO ON. WITH A TOP DRIVER AND A CAR THAT'S JUST RIGHT, I'M SURE WE'LL HAVE A WINNING TEAM.

I WANT YOU TO BE TEAM LOTUS'S LEAD DRIVER. WE'LL DO EVERYTHING TO GET YOU WINNING!

OK, COLIN, I ACCEPT!

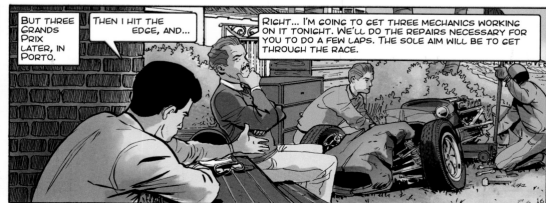

BUT THREE GRANDS PRIX LATER, IN PORTO.

THEN I HIT THE EDGE, AND...

RIGHT... I'M GOING TO GET THREE MECHANICS WORKING ON IT TONIGHT. WE'LL DO THE REPAIRS NECESSARY FOR YOU TO DO A FEW LAPS. THE SOLE AIM WILL BE TO GET THROUGH THE RACE.

THE CHASSIS HAS BEEN EXTENSIVELY RE-WELDED, THE BODYWORK IS PATCHED UP WITH STICKY TAPE, BUT WE'VE NO IDEA WHETHER IT'S GOING TO HOLD.

DO A FEW TEST LAPS BEFORE YOU GO ON THE ATTACK, BUT DON'T PUSH THINGS TOO HARD!

RIGHT.

AS THE RACE GOES ON...

THIS CAR IS HANDLING QUITE NICELY!

SO WELL, IN FACT, THAT CLARK FINISHES IN THIRD PLACE, HIS BEST RESULT OF THE SEASON!

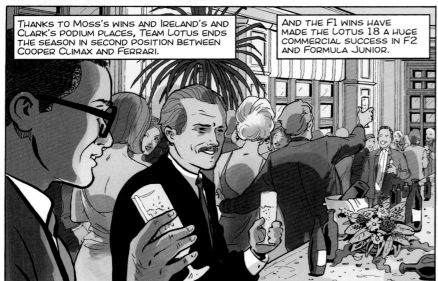

THANKS TO MOSS'S WINS AND IRELAND'S AND CLARK'S PODIUM PLACES, TEAM LOTUS ENDS THE SEASON IN SECOND POSITION BETWEEN COOPER CLIMAX AND FERRARI.

AND THE F1 WINS HAVE MADE THE LOTUS 18 A HUGE COMMERCIAL SUCCESS IN F2 AND FORMULA JUNIOR.

WE'VE GOT A FEW WEEKS LEFT TO GET READY FOR THE 1961 SEASON. I'M SURE THAT AS SOON AS WE CAN GET HOLD OF THE CLIMAX V8 THAT CONFORMS TO THE NEW RULES, THE TITLE WILL BE WITHIN OUR GRASP.

TO OUR FUTURE SUCCESS!

17

It's 1961 and there are new rules on engines. Maximum capacity is reduced to 1,500cc, to the displeasure of the English constructors, who aren't prepared for it. Chapman is waiting for Climax's new FWMV V8. In the meantime, the new Lotus 21 is given the four-cylinder FPF already used in Formula 2. But with only 155bhp, it lacks punch compared with the 190bhp of Ferrari's V6.

The season is dominated by Phil Hill and Wolfgang von Trips in their Ferrari Dino 156 cars. Team Lotus proves incapable of battling its way to victory.

monaco
3e GRAND PRIX JUNIOR
et XIXe GRAND PRIX AUTOMOBILE

Ferrari 156:
Ferrari V6 (120°)
1,476cc, 190bhp at 9,500rpm
Two valves per cylinder, four OHC
Five-speed gearbox
Tubular steel chassis
460kg

At Monaco, where power isn't so decisive, Moss's skill decides the race. He drives a Lotus 18, Chapman having refused to sell Rob Walker a 21. To avoid any risk of overheating, the side panels have been removed.

This initial Grand Prix of the season is a disaster for Team Lotus. The two new 21s are wrecked in qualifying. Ireland breaks his leg and Clark finishes only tenth.

WE'VE ONLY GOT A WEEK TO REBUILD THE CARS.

TREVOR TAYLOR WILL REPLACE IRELAND FOR A FEW RACES.

CHAPMAN GOES FROM ONE DISAPPOINTMENT TO ANOTHER IN THE ENSUING GPs.

THE ITALIAN GP AT MONZA. ON THE FIRST LAP, AS THEY BRAKE FOR PARABOLICA, CLARK ATTACKS VON TRIPS, WHO FAILS TO SEE HIM.

HEY...

THE TWO CARS TOUCH EACH OTHER...

THE FERRARI FLIES OVER THE BANK BEFORE PLUNGING INTO THE CROWD, KILLING 14 PEOPLE. THROWN OUT OF HIS CAR, VON TRIPS IS KILLED TOO. CLARK IS UNSCATHED. THE EMERGENCY TEAMS GET TO WORK AS THE RACE CONTINUES. PHIL HILL WINS THE RACE AND IS CROWNED WORLD CHAMPION. FERRARI TAKES THE CONSTRUCTORS' TITLE.

18

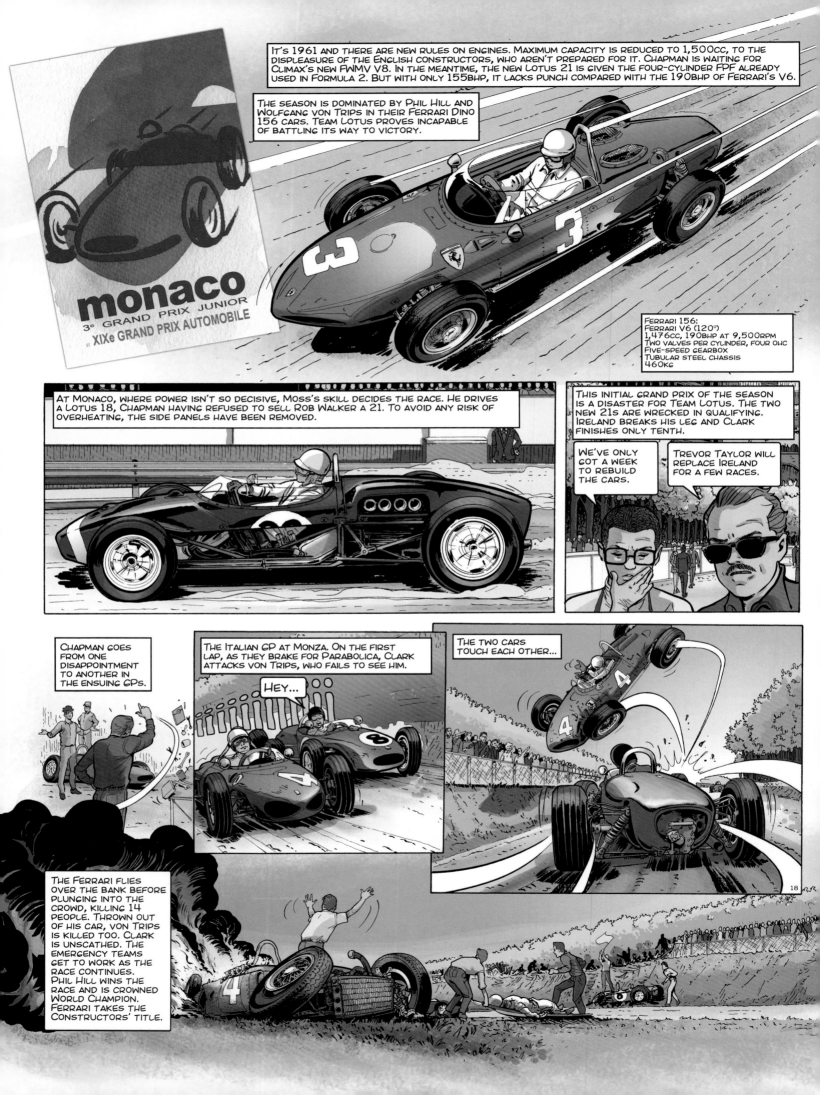

THE UNITED STATES GRAND PRIX AT WATKINS GLEN. TEAM LOTUS FINALLY WINS ITS FIRST GRAND PRIX, THANKS TO INNES IRELAND, WHILE THE FERRARIS ARE ABSENT. CLARK FINISHES ONLY SEVENTH THANKS TO CLUTCH PROBLEMS.

YOU'VE GOT YOUR FIRST WIN, COLIN!

KNOWING INNES, HE WON'T BE SLEEPING MUCH TONIGHT...

TEAM LOTUS FINISHES THE '61 SEASON IN SECOND PLACE IN THE CONSTRUCTORS' CHAMPIONSHIP.

A LITTLE LATER, AT THE LONDON SHOW...

GOOD TO SEE YOU HERE! BY THE WAY, YOU STILL HAVEN'T SAID ANYTHING ABOUT MY CONTRACT FOR NEXT SEASON!

I'M SORRY, INNES, I DON'T HAVE A PLACE FOR YOU. I WON'T BE NEEDING YOUR SERVICES!

WHAT? COME ON COLIN!

I'VE DECIDED TO ENTRUST MY CARS TO CLARK AND TAYLOR. JIM IS VERY FAST AND HAS A METHODICAL APPROACH TO PREPARATION AND THE RACE ITSELF. AT HIS AGE, HE LOOKS TO HAVE A PROMISING FUTURE...

CLARK? BUT I WAS AHEAD OF HIM PRACTICALLY THE WHOLE SEASON!

HE HAS A LIFE STYLE IN KEEPING WITH WHAT I EXPECT FROM A PROFESSIONAL DRIVER... AND TREVOR WILL MAKE A GOOD NUMBER TWO. SORRY, INNES.

SO THAT'S HOW YOU THANK ME FOR BRINGING YOU YOUR FIRST F1 WIN! AND FOR DRIVING YOUR COFFINS ON WHEELS WITHOUT A SINGLE COMPLAINT! THANKS, COLIN!

GENTLEMEN, IF TEAM LOTUS IS TO STEAL A LEAD OVER THE COMPETITION, WE'RE GOING TO HAVE TO INNOVATE!

ANNABEL LEE TAVERN

Restaurant

POLICE BOX

FOR HIRE

EDU 58

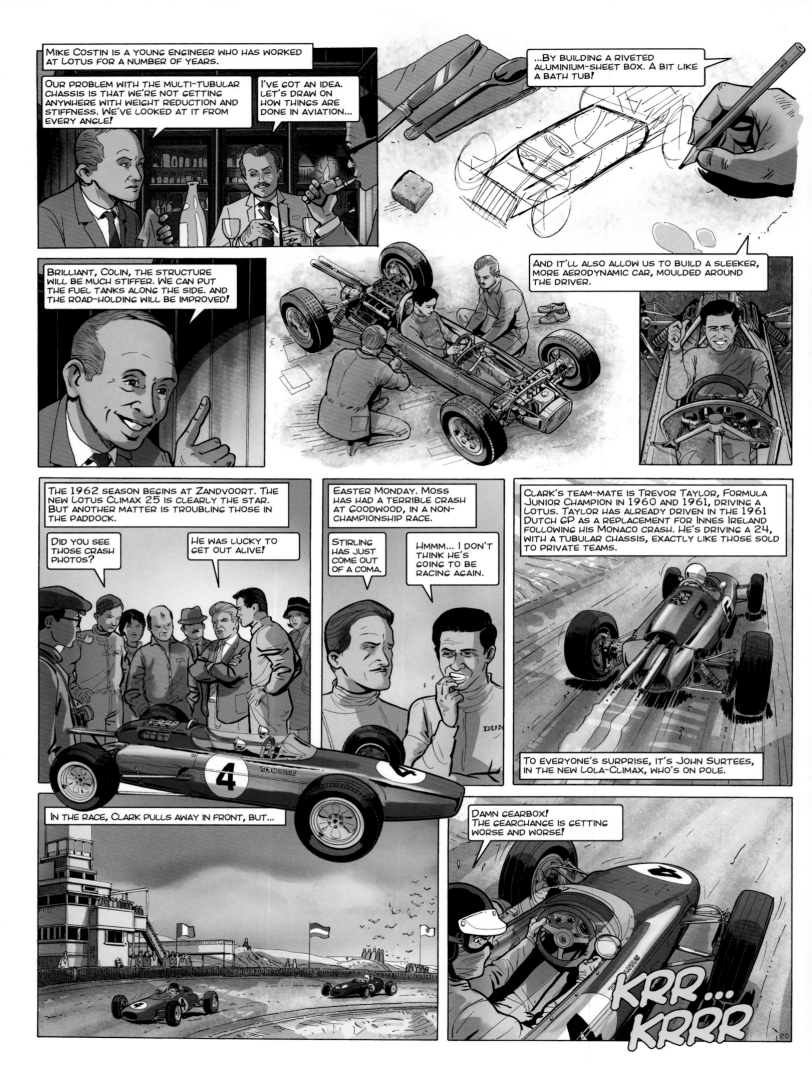

MIKE COSTIN IS A YOUNG ENGINEER WHO HAS WORKED AT LOTUS FOR A NUMBER OF YEARS.

OUR PROBLEM WITH THE MULTI-TUBULAR CHASSIS IS THAT WE'RE NOT GETTING ANYWHERE WITH WEIGHT REDUCTION AND STIFFNESS. WE'VE LOOKED AT IT FROM EVERY ANGLE!

I'VE GOT AN IDEA. LET'S DRAW ON HOW THINGS ARE DONE IN AVIATION...

...BY BUILDING A RIVETED ALUMINIUM-SHEET BOX. A BIT LIKE A BATH TUB!

BRILLIANT, COLIN, THE STRUCTURE WILL BE MUCH STIFFER. WE CAN PUT THE FUEL TANKS ALONG THE SIDE. AND THE ROAD-HOLDING WILL BE IMPROVED!

AND IT'LL ALSO ALLOW US TO BUILD A SLEEKER, MORE AERODYNAMIC CAR, MOULDED AROUND THE DRIVER.

THE 1962 SEASON BEGINS AT ZANDVOORT. THE NEW LOTUS CLIMAX 25 IS CLEARLY THE STAR. BUT ANOTHER MATTER IS TROUBLING THOSE IN THE PADDOCK.

DID YOU SEE THOSE CRASH PHOTOS?

HE WAS LUCKY TO GET OUT ALIVE!

EASTER MONDAY. MOSS HAS HAD A TERRIBLE CRASH AT GOODWOOD, IN A NON-CHAMPIONSHIP RACE.

STIRLING HAS JUST COME OUT OF A COMA.

HMMM... I DON'T THINK HE'S GOING TO BE RACING AGAIN.

CLARK'S TEAM-MATE IS TREVOR TAYLOR, FORMULA JUNIOR CHAMPION IN 1960 AND 1961, DRIVING A LOTUS. TAYLOR HAS ALREADY DRIVEN IN THE 1961 DUTCH GP AS A REPLACEMENT FOR INNES IRELAND FOLLOWING HIS MONACO CRASH. HE'S DRIVING A 24, WITH A TUBULAR CHASSIS, EXACTLY LIKE THOSE SOLD TO PRIVATE TEAMS.

TO EVERYONE'S SURPRISE, IT'S JOHN SURTEES, IN THE NEW LOLA-CLIMAX, WHO'S ON POLE.

IN THE RACE, CLARK PULLS AWAY IN FRONT, BUT...

DAMN GEARBOX! THE GEARCHANGE IS GETTING WORSE AND WORSE!

KRR... KRRR

AND IT'S GRAHAM HILL WHO TAKES HIS FIRST GRAND PRIX WIN, IN THE BRM.

BRM P578: BRM ENGINE, V8 (90°), 1,498CC, TWIN OHC, TWO VALVES PER CYLINDER, 192BHP AT 10,500RPM, FIVE-SPEED GEARBOX TUBULAR STEEL CHASSIS, 490KG

TREVOR TAYLOR COMES AWAY WITH AN EXCELLENT SECOND PLACE! CLARK, HAMPERED BY HIS GEARBOX PROBLEMS, FINISHES TENTH.

AN AMAZING PERFORMANCE, TREVOR!

THAT SHOULD BOOST SALES TO PRIVATEERS...

IT'S GOING TO BE A HELL OF A BATTLE WITH THE BRM LADS THIS YEAR!

AT MONACO, TEAM LOTUS SUFFERS A DOUBLE RETIREMENT. THE SEASON'S THIRD GP IS AT SPA.

IN QUALIFYING, CLARK IS FACED WITH A BLOWN ENGINE.

WE'RE GOING TO HAVE TO SEND YOUR V8 BACK TO COVENTRY. A MECHANIC WILL DO THE ROUND TRIP. BUT TAYLOR'S ENGINE IS RUNNING LIKE CLOCKWORK. HE'LL BE ON THE FRONT ROW, NEXT TO HILL AND MCLAREN.

FRANCORCHAMPS
17 JUIN – 15 HEURES
GRAND PRIX DE BELGIQUE
Tombola gratuite les sports
1er Prix : une "DAUPHINE 1093"

I REALLY HATE THIS CIRCUIT... AND IT'S PAYING ME BACK.

GOD KNOWS WHAT TRAGEDY WE'LL SEE THIS YEAR!

CLARK STARTS THE RACE AT THE BACK OF THE GRID IN 16TH PLACE.

21

By the time he rounds 'La Source' on the first lap, Clark is already fourth.

He smashes lap record after lap record!

...AND WINS THE GRAND PRIX 44 SECONDS AHEAD OF GRAHAM HILL'S BRM AND MORE THAN TWO MINUTES AHEAD OF THE WORLD CHAMPION, PHIL HILL, IN HIS FERRARI!

JIM HAD BEEN WAITING TWO YEARS FOR THIS FIRST WIN!

AND I'M SURE THERE'LL BE MANY OTHERS!

THE GEARBOX JAMMED AND I WAS HIT BY MAIRESSE, BUT IT'S A WASTE OF TIME TALKING TO COLIN ABOUT IT. AS USUAL, HE'S ONLY GOT TIME FOR CLARK!

JIMMY, LET ME HUG YOU. I'M SO HAPPY!

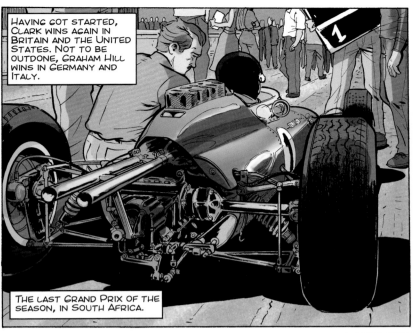

HAVING GOT STARTED, CLARK WINS AGAIN IN BRITAIN AND THE UNITED STATES. NOT TO BE OUTDONE, GRAHAM HILL WINS IN GERMANY AND ITALY.

THE LAST GRAND PRIX OF THE SEASON, IN SOUTH AFRICA.

WHAT'S BOTHERING YOU ON A DAY LIKE THIS?

PEOPLE LIKE YOU WHO KEEP ASKING ME STUPID QUESTIONS!

THE RULES ARE SIMPLE: WHICHEVER ONE OF US WINS WILL TAKE THE WORLD CHAMPIONSHIP.

STRAIGHT AWAY, CLARK LEADS THIS HOTLY CONTESTED RACE.

WE'RE HALFWAY THROUGH AND JIMMY IS 30 SECONDS AHEAD OF HILL. IT'S ALL GOING VERY WELL.

COLIN, LOOK!

CLARK'S ENGINE...

QUICK, GET READY, HE'S PROBABLY GOING TO STOP ON THE NEXT LAP!

THE ENGINE'S COVERED IN OIL!

A BOLT IN THE TIMING-CHAIN CASE HAS FAILED.

WE CAN'T GO ON!

FOR THE THIRD YEAR RUNNING, TEAM LOTUS IS SECOND IN THE CONSTRUCTORS' CHAMPIONSHIP!

JABBY, WE'RE JINXED!

COME ON, COLIN. I BET YOU WE'LL BE CHAMPIONS NEXT SEASON!

COLIN, WHY DON'T YOU TAKE SOME LESSONS FROM BRM AND LEARN HOW TO TIGHTEN BOLTS PROPERLY!

23

1963

The year 1963 finally bears fruit. The Lotus Climax 25 is perfectly set up. Clark shows his credentials as the man to beat right from the first Grand Prix, at Monaco. But gearbox problems allow Graham Hill to take the race in his BRM. Jim then has successive wins at Spa, Zandvoort, Rheims and Silverstone. He finishes second at the Nürburgring and wins again at Monza.

24

With seven wins from ten Grand Prix races, Clark takes the Drivers' World Championship and brings Team Lotus its much-coveted Constructors' title. Chapman is in seventh heaven!

In just ten years, Chapman has achieved his aim of making Lotus a benchmark in F1 among such great names as Ferrari, BRM and Cooper.

JUST THINK HOW FAR WE'VE COME, HAZEL!

I TOLD YOU WE'D DO IT!

DO YOU REMEMBER HOW MY FATHER OBJECTED WHEN I TOLD HIM THAT I WANTED TO GIVE UP MY JOB AT THE BRITISH ALUMINIUM COMPANY...?

I MOST CERTAINLY DO!

LATE 1954.

LOOK, DAD, THE ORDER BOOK FOR NEXT YEAR IS FULL. IT'S THE RIGHT MOMENT!

The Railway Hotel

COLIN, YOU'RE A TALENTED ENGINEER! I'M TELLING YOU: THINK OF YOUR FUTURE!

BUT DAD, THE FUTURE IS IN CARS. I'VE MADE MY DECISION!

WHAT DECISION? TO MAKE SMALL CARS FOR SOME SO-CALLED SPORTSMEN WHO ARE JUST GOING TO SIT AT THE WHEEL DRIVING IN CIRCLES GOING 'BRROOM, BRROOM'!

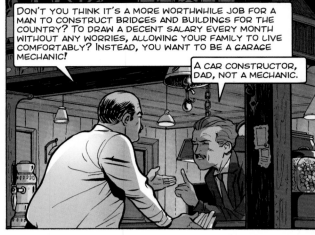

DON'T YOU THINK IT'S A MORE WORTHWHILE JOB FOR A MAN TO CONSTRUCT BRIDGES AND BUILDINGS FOR THE COUNTRY? TO DRAW A DECENT SALARY EVERY MONTH WITHOUT ANY WORRIES, ALLOWING YOUR FAMILY TO LIVE COMFORTABLY? INSTEAD, YOU WANT TO BE A GARAGE MECHANIC!

A CAR CONSTRUCTOR, DAD, NOT A MECHANIC.

AND THANKS TO MY WINS, I'LL BE A FAMOUS DRIVER...

HUH! ENOUGH OF THIS RIDICULOUS NONSENSE!

YOU WAIT AND SEE, LOTUS WILL BE A GREAT NAME IN MOTOR RACING.

WHAT? WITH THOSE RABBIT HUTCHES YOU MESS AROUND WITH AT THE BACK OF MY PUB? YOU MUST BE JOKING! DO YOU SERIOUSLY EXPECT TO PROVIDE FOR YOUR FAMILY DOING THAT?

HAZEL BACKS ME! SHE BELIEVES IN ME AT LEAST!

HORNSEY, 1955. FRED BUSHELL HAS JUST LEFT A LUCRATIVE JOB IN THE CITY TO JOIN LOTUS. OVER THE YEARS, AS DIRECTOR OF FINANCE AND ADMINISTRATION, HE WOULD ORGANISE LOTUS INTO THREE GROUPS: PRODUCTION CARS, RACING CARS BUILT FOR CUSTOMERS, AND CARS RACING FOR THE COMPANY.

COULD YOU JUST SIGN THIS CONTRACT, COLIN? I'VE READ IT THROUGH. THERE'S NO PROBLEM.

THANKS, FRED. I'M LUCKY TO HAVE YOU HERE!

IT'S TIME TO THINK ABOUT THE GROUP'S STRATEGY.

YOU KNOW AS WELL AS I DO THAT RACING CAR SALES ARE TOO SEASONAL AND SPORADIC TO GUARANTEE ENOUGH FINANCE TO SUPPORT DEVELOPMENT AND FUND OUR RACING ACTIVITIES.

YES. I READ YOUR MEMO. I AGREE. IT'S JUST NOT ENOUGH!

I DON'T KNOW WHAT TO DO...

LOOK AT MG.

THEY USE THEIR PRESENCE IN RACING TO SELL PRODUCTION CARS. IT WORKS VERY WELL!

IT'S TRUE THEY'VE HAD A LOT OF COMMERCIAL SUCCESS WITH THEIR NEW MGA.

WHY NOT COME UP WITH A SPORTS CAR, A GT? THE MARKET IS EXPANDING ALL THE TIME.

EXCELLENT IDEA, FRED. A CAR YOU COULD USE EQUALLY WELL FOR GOING TO WORK OR GOING IN FOR THE MONTE CARLO RALLY OR LE MANS.

I ALSO THINK WE SHOULD DO AN UPDATED AND MORE REFINED VERSION OF OUR Mk VI.

YES, SOME CUSTOMERS HAVE ALREADY ASKED ME FOR THAT! THE TWO PROJECTS WILL GUARANTEE US A REGULAR TURNOVER AND THE PROFITS WILL PAY FOR OUR RACING TEAM.

AT THE 1957 LONDON MOTOR SHOW, LOTUS DISPLAYS TWO NEW MODELS: THE SEVEN, DERIVED FROM THE Mk VI; AND THE ELITE, AN ATTRACTIVE GT WITH AN INNOVATIVE GLASS-FIBRE BODY.

LOTUS SEVEN F:
FORD 100E ENGINE
FOUR CYLINDERS IN LINE, 1,172CC
SINGLE CAMSHAFT, TWO SIDE VALVES PER CYLINDER
48BHP AT 4,500RPM
THREE-SPEED GEARBOX
TUBULAR STEEL CHASSIS
ALUMINIUM BODYWORK
445KG

— *the build-it-yourself sports car*

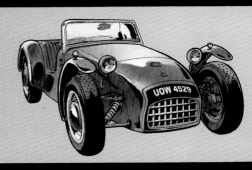

Brilliant new offspring of the mighty Lotus racers!

LOTUS ELITE:
CLIMAX FWE ENGINE, FOUR CYLINDERS IN LINE, 1,216CC
SINGLE OHC, TWO VALVES PER CYLINDER, 75BHP AT 6,100RPM
FOUR-SPEED GEARBOX, GLASS-FIBRE MONOCOQUE, 600KG

AND, IN 1959, TO CATER FOR THE COMMERCIAL SUCCESS OF THE SEVEN AND THE ELITE...

LOTUS MOVES INTO NEW PREMISES AT CHESHUNT, NORTH LONDON.

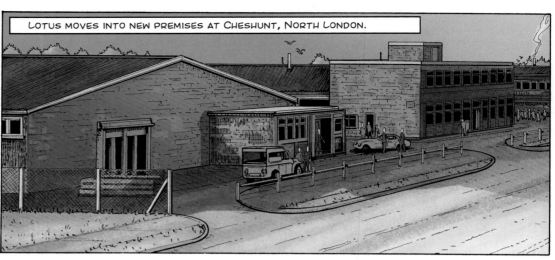

BY 1962, PRODUCTION OF CARS FOR RACING CUSTOMERS IS EXPANDING, AND THERE ARE SUCCESSES IN BOTH EUROPE AND THE USA.

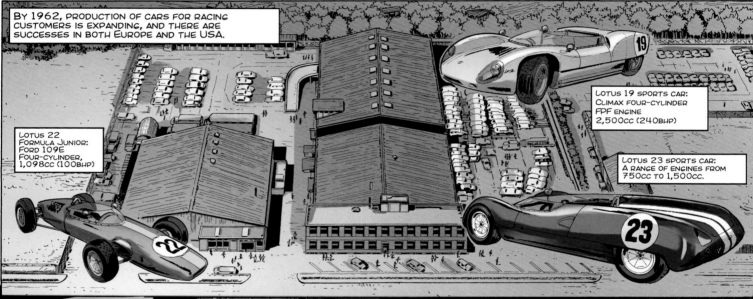

LOTUS 22 FORMULA JUNIOR: FORD 109E FOUR-CYLINDER, 1,098cc (100BHP)

LOTUS 19 SPORTS CAR: CLIMAX FOUR-CYLINDER FPF ENGINE 2,500cc (240BHP)

LOTUS 23 SPORTS CAR: A RANGE OF ENGINES FROM 750cc TO 1,500cc.

IN THE SAME YEAR, THE ELAN REPLACES THE ELITE AND, ON THE BACK OF CLARK'S LOTUS WINS, ACHIEVES EVEN GREATER COMMERCIAL SUCCESS.

"I drive my lotus for pleasure-not because I have to" says World Champion jim Clark

EMMA PEEL, THE UNCONVENTIONAL HEROINE OF 'THE AVENGERS', EXCLUSIVELY DRIVES A LOTUS ELAN, A SYMBOL OF BRITAIN'S TECHNOLOGICAL SUPREMACY.

LOTUS ELAN S1: FORD TWIN-CAM ENGINE FOUR CYLINDERS IN LINE, 1,558cc TWIN OHC, TWO VALVES PER CYLINDER 105BHP AT 5,500RPM FOUR-SPEED GEARBOX GIRDER CHASSIS, GLASS-FIBRE BODYWORK, 680KG

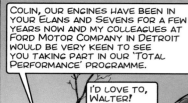

COLIN, OUR ENGINES HAVE BEEN IN YOUR ELANS AND SEVENS FOR A FEW YEARS NOW AND MY COLLEAGUES AT FORD MOTOR COMPANY IN DETROIT WOULD BE VERY KEEN TO SEE YOU TAKING PART IN OUR 'TOTAL PERFORMANCE' PROGRAMME.

I'D LOVE TO, WALTER!

OUR STRATEGY IS CLEAR: WE'RE AIMING TO WIN BOTH LE MANS AND INDIANAPOLIS, AND PERHAPS, ONE DAY, IN F1, TOO!

WALTER, I HAVE A FEW IDEAS FOR TURNING THE FORD CORTINA INTO A PROPER LITTLE ROCKET!

THE LOTUS CORTINA DRIVEN BY JIM CLARK HAS A STRING OF ENGLISH TOURING-CAR CHAMPIONSHIP WINS IN 1964. ITS FORD 1.6-LITRE TWIN-CAM ENGINE DEVELOPED BY COSWORTH HOLDS UP WELL AGAINST THE HUGE 7-LITRE V8 GALAXIES.

1963. WALTER HAYES IS FORD UK'S DYNAMIC PUBLIC RELATIONS MANAGER.

IT WAS ENOUGH TO COMPENSATE FOR A DISAPPOINTING SEASON IN F1, ONE THAT ENDED WITH THIRD PLACE IN THE WORLD CHAMPIONSHIP FOR BOTH CLARK AND LOTUS CLIMAX.

LOTUS CORTINA Mk1:
FORD COSWORTH ENGINE, FOUR CYLINDERS IN LINE, 1,558cc, TWIN OHC, TWO VALVES PER CYLINDER, 105BHP AT 5,500RPM, FOUR-SPEED GEARBOX, STEEL BODYWORK, 950KG

1 JANUARY 1965, SOUTH AFRICAN GRAND PRIX, EAST LONDON.

JIMMY, HOW'S YOUR BACK?

IT'LL BE OK, THANKS TO THE TRUSS... GOOD ENOUGH TO TAKE POLE ANYWAY.

THAT WINTER, DURING A LOTUS CORTINA PUBLICITY EVENT, CLARK HAD MANAGED TO INJURE HIS BACK... IN A SNOWBALL FIGHT!

JIM, YOU'VE BEEN HEAD AND SHOULDERS ABOVE YOUR TEAM-MATES FOR YEARS. LET'S HOPE SPENCE WILL DO BETTER. HE'S HAD SOME VERY GOOD RESULTS IN FORMULA JUNIOR AND F2!

THE LOTUS 33 IS NOW PERFECTLY SET UP.

BEHIND CLARK'S LOTUS IS REIGNING CHAMPION JOHN SURTEES'S FERRARI...

AND THE OLD ENEMY: GRAHAM HILL IN HIS BRM.

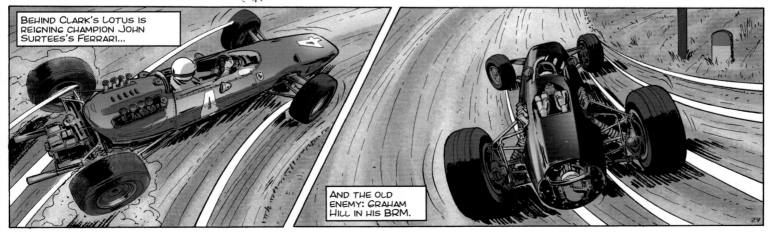

AND AT THE FINISH OF THE FIRST GRAND PRIX OF 1965...

CLARK COMES HOME WELL AHEAD OF SURTEES, HILL AND SPENCE.

WE'RE OFF TO A GOOD START!

AND FOLLOWING SOUTH AFRICA, THE SCOTSMAN CHALKS UP WINS AT SPA, CLERMONT-FERRAND, SILVERSTONE AND ZANDVOORT.

WHICH NEWSPAPER DO YOU WORK FOR, HANNA?

THE 'FRANKFURTER ALLGEMEINE ZEITUNG'. IT'S ONE OF THE BIG DAILIES. I'D LIKE TO DO A BEHIND-THE-SCENES ARTICLE ON F1 AND LOTUS.

THAT'S GREAT! I'LL START OFF BY INTRODUCING YOU TO THE TEAM. THERE AREN'T MANY OF US.

WE HAVE FOUR MECHANICS FOR EITHER TWO OR THREE CARS, DEPENDING ON THE RACE.

THERE'S OUR CHIEF MECHANIC, WHO'S CHECKING JIM'S CAR. OUR FANTASTIC DRIVER HAS AGAIN CLINCHED POLE AHEAD OF HILL'S BRM!

LET'S NOT DISTURB THEM.

THIS WEEKEND, OUR THIRD CAR IS BEING DRIVEN BY A YOUNG GERMAN, GERHARD MITTER. IT'S A LOTUS 25. IT SHOULD BRING IN A BIT OF EXTRA MONEY – OUR BUDGET IS TIGHT.

EVERYTHING ALL RIGHT, LADS?

WITH EACH RACE, WE'RE JUGGLING THE MONEY TO COVER THE MECHANICS, SPARE PARTS, TRAVEL, HOTEL EXPENSES... WE GET AROUND £3,000* A RACE. IT'S NOT ENOUGH TO LIVE IN LUXURY!

*EQUIVALENT TO ABOUT £43,000 TODAY.

LUCKILY, OUR WINS HAVE ALLOWED US TO GET A GOOD DEAL ON ENGINES FROM OUR PARTNERS, COVENTRY CLIMAX.

LET'S GO TO THE PITS. THAT'S WHERE WE WATCH THE RACE. OUR FRIEND CROMBAC, A COLLEAGUE OF YOURS WHO STARTED THE MAGAZINE 'SPORT AUTO' IN FRANCE, IS THE ONE WHO TIMES THE CARS AND SUPERVISES THE PIT STOPS.

BEHIND CLARK ARE HILL IN THE BRM AND GURNEY'S BRABHAM.

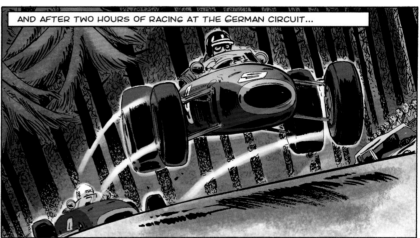

AND AFTER TWO HOURS OF RACING AT THE GERMAN CIRCUIT...

...IT'S ANOTHER GRAND SLAM FOR CLARK WHO, AFTER TAKING POLE, LED THE GP FROM START TO FINISH AND SET THE FASTEST LAP.

IT'S A RESULT THAT BRINGS CLARK A SECOND DRIVERS' WORLD CHAMPIONSHIP AND LOTUS A SECOND CONSTRUCTORS' TITLE WITH THREE RACES STILL TO GO.

31

POST-RACE, THE CHRISTOPHORUS RESTAURANT.

MY FRIENDS, I RAISE MY GLASS TO THE YEAR 1965, WHICH HAS BROUGHT US SO MUCH SUCCESS. I WANT TO THANK YOU FOR ALL YOUR EFFORTS AND FOR THE QUALITY OF YOUR WORK.

I'D PARTICULARLY LIKE TO THANK OUR NUMBER ONE DRIVER, WITHOUT WHOM ALL THOSE WINS WOULDN'T HAVE BEEN POSSIBLE. THANK YOU JIMMY, AND YOUR GOOD HEALTH!

BECAUSE, YOU KNOW, WE WON NOT ONLY THE DOUBLE OF DRIVERS' AND CONSTRUCTORS' TITLES WITH CLIMAX...

...BUT ALSO THE INDIANAPOLIS 500 WITH FORD!

FANTASTIC, JIMMY, YOU EXCEEDED 160MPH! YOU'RE FAR AND AWAY THE QUICKEST IN QUALIFYING. IT'S A GREAT START!

WE'RE GOING TO HAVE TO KEEP AN EYE ON FOYT AND GURNEY. WE'LL ADAPT OUR PIT STOPS ACCORDING TO THEIR STRATEGY AND WHATEVER INTERRUPTIONS OCCUR IN THE RACE. AND WE NEED TO BE CAREFUL TOWARDS THE END SO THAT WE SAVE FUEL.

RIGHT FROM THE START, CLARK TAKES THE LEAD!

VROOOOOOO
VROOOOOOO
VROOOOOOO

HE IS CHASED BY THE TWO LOTUSES OF FOYT AND GURNEY.

BROAAAA
BROAAAA

32

AFTER 67 LAPS, CLARK HAS TO REFUEL AND CHANGE TYRES, AND HANDS THE LEAD TO FOYT.

CHAPMAN HIRED THE WOOD BROTHERS TO HANDLE THE PIT STOPS. THEY'RE THE QUICKEST PITCREW IN THE NASCAR PADDOCK AND CLARK SETS OFF AGAIN WITH NEW TYRES AND A FULL FUEL LOAD AFTER A MUCH SHORTER STOP THAN THE OPPOSITION.

CLARK MOVES UP INTO THE LEAD. BY THE END, HE'LL HAVE LED IN 190 OF THE 200 LAPS, WINNING AT A RECORD AVERAGE OF JUST OVER 150MPH!

IT'S THE FIRST TIME SINCE 1916 THAT AMERICAN DRIVERS HAVE BEEN BEATEN BY A FOREIGNER. IT'S ALSO A FIRST WIN FOR A REAR-ENGINED CAR. CLARK, CHAPMAN AND THE TEAM ARE JUSTLY PROUD. AND FORD HAVE THEIR MUCH-COVETED VICTORY

LOTUS 38:
FORD V8 ENGINE (90°)
4,195CC, TWIN OHC
FOUR VALVES PER CYLINDER,
505BHP AT 8,400RPM
ZF TWO-SPEED GEARBOX
ALUMINIUM MONOCOQUE CHASSIS
TOTAL WEIGHT 612KG

THIS RESULT WILL INCREASE SALES FOR OUR AMERICAN DEALERS... THERE'S NOT A SINGLE CAR IN THE USA THAT CAN COMPETE DIRECTLY WITH OUR ELANS!

OK JIMMY, LET'S GO! WE'VE JUST GOT TIME TO CATCH THE PLANE FOR THE NEXT RACE! NO TIME TO HANG AROUND!

33

NO MATTER WHICH COUNTRY HE'S IN, CLARK KEEPS WINNING.

ROAAAAAAW

CLARK REGAINS MOTOR RACING CHAMPIONSHIP

GERMAN GRAND PRIX BRINGS HIM SIXTH SUCCESSIVE WIN ! Jim Clark, a 29-year-old scottish sheep farmer and leader or Britain's Lotus team, won the twenty-seventh German Grand Prix here today - his sixth successive grand prix ...tory - and in

MR CHAPMAN, THIS YEAR YOU'VE TAKEN A SECOND FORMULA 1 CONSTRUCTORS' TITLE, AND ALSO WON THE INDIANAPOLIS 500, THE FRENCH FORMULA 2 CHAMPIONSHIP AND THE TASMAN SERIES, NOT TO MENTION NUMEROUS VICTORIES IN OTHER CATEGORIES ALL OVER THE GLOBE! TO WHAT DO YOU ATTRIBUTE THIS EXTRAORDINARY SUCCESS?

WELL, HANNA, WE'VE LEARNED A LOT FROM OUR EARLIER EXPERIENCES. WE'VE IMPROVED RELIABILITY, THANKS TO AN EVER MORE PROFESSIONAL TEAM. BUT NONE OF IT WOULD HAVE BEEN POSSIBLE WITHOUT JIMMY'S INCREDIBLE TALENT!

YOUR ROAD CARS ARE ALSO VERY SUCCESSFUL COMMERCIALLY...

YES... WE'RE NOW BUILDING AROUND 2,000 CARS A YEAR. THEY'RE SOLD THROUGHOUT THE WORLD. THIS IS OUR LATEST MODEL: THE ELAN S2.

BUT, FOR ME, THE MOST IMPORTANT THING IS THAT LOTUS IS STEADILY BECOMING THE TOP NAME IN MOTOR RACING.

SO, YOU'RE A KIND OF ENGLISH ENZO FERRARI?

WELL, WITH ONE DIFFERENCE! FERRARI IS 67...

AND YOU ARE 37!

WOULD YOU JUST STAND THERE? I'D LIKE A PHOTO IN FRONT OF THE HOUSE.

AUGUST 1965, AT CHESHUNT.

COLIN? ARE THINGS OK?

JABBY, ER... YES... I WAS LOST IN THOUGHT... WE'VE GOT A BIG PROBLEM!

THE FIA HAS DECIDED TO INCREASE ENGINE CAPACITY TO 3 LITRES FOR NEXT SEASON... DAMN IT, JUST AS WE'VE GOT OUR 1,500 RUNNING RELIABLY! WHAT ARE WE GOING TO DO?

BUT COVENTRY CLIMAX...

CLIMAX HAS JUST BEEN BOUGHT BY JAGUAR. THEY'VE DECIDED TO PULL OUT OF RACING AFTER USING THEIR ENGINES IN OUR CARS FOR YEARS! I DON'T HAVE THE MEANS TO BUILD MY OWN ENGINES!

WHAT ABOUT FINDING ANOTHER ENGINE MAKER?

I DON'T SEE MYSELF CONTACTING FERRARI OR MASERATI! OR HONDA! THERE'S JUST BRM. I'VE HEARD THAT TONY RUDD IS WORKING ON A 16-CYLINDER ENGINE!

I THINK THE BEST THING WOULD BE TO ASK MIKE COSTIN AND KEITH DUCKWORTH TO BUILD AN ENGINE FOR US.

BUT HOW WOULD WE FINANCE THE DEVELOPMENT OF A NEW COSWORTH ENGINE?

I'LL SPEAK TO TONY RUDD AND KEITH DUCKWORTH TO ARRANGE A MEETING!

THIS IS JUST THE SORT OF PROJECT THAT WOULD APPEAL TO FORD AND OUR FRIEND WALTER HAYES!

A BRILLIANT AIRCRAFT ENGINE SPECIALIST, TONY RUDD HAD PUT ALL HIS ENGINEERING EXPERIENCE AT BRM'S DISPOSAL WHEN HE JOINED THEM IN THE EARLY 1950s.

YOU KNOW OUR 1.5-LITRE V8 THAT WE'VE BEEN USING FOR THREE YEARS. IT'S A PARTICULARLY POWERFUL ENGINE THANKS TO ITS SHORT STROKE ALLOWING HIGH REVS TO BE REACHED. IT WAS A BIG FACTOR IN BRM'S AND GRAHAM HILL'S DOUBLE TITLE WIN IN 1962...

TONY, DON'T RUB IT IN...

THE AIM FOR OUR NEXT ENGINE IS TO ACHIEVE RELIABILITY BY USING AS MANY PARTS OF THE V8 AS POSSIBLE.

YOU MEAN HEADS, PISTONS, CON RODS, VALVES, CRANKSHAFTS AND SO ON?

EXACTLY! MY IDEA IS TO RETAIN ALL OF ITS OVERALL FEATURES AND PUT TOGETHER TWO 1,500CC V8s TO GIVE A 3-LITRE 16-CYLINDER ENGINE.

BUT A V16 WOULD MAKE THE ENGINE MUCH TOO LONG FOR A MODERN F1 CAR...

ABSOLUTELY! SO MY IDEA, AS USED IN AVIATION, IS AN H-SHAPED ENGINE, ON ITS SIDE, WITH EIGHT LEFT-HAND AND EIGHT RIGHT-HAND CYLINDERS. THE TWO CRANKSHAFTS ARE ARRANGED ONE OVER THE OTHER AND LINKED BY A GEAR TRAIN. IN SHORT, A PIECE OF JEWELLERY!

I'M AFRAID IT MIGHT BE OVER-COMPLICATED...!

TONY, WHAT POWER DO YOU THINK YOU'LL GET OUT OF THIS ENGINE?

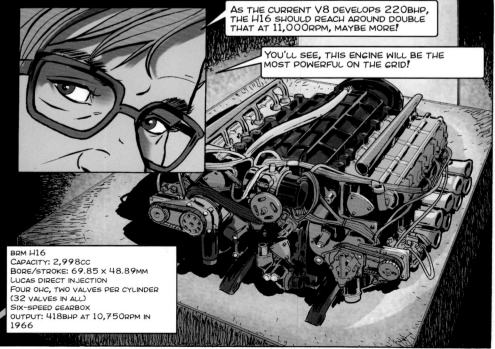

AS THE CURRENT V8 DEVELOPS 220BHP, THE H16 SHOULD REACH AROUND DOUBLE THAT AT 11,000RPM, MAYBE MORE!

YOU'LL SEE, THIS ENGINE WILL BE THE MOST POWERFUL ON THE GRID!

BRM H16
CAPACITY: 2,998CC
BORE/STROKE: 69.85 x 48.89MM
LUCAS DIRECT INJECTION
FOUR OHC, TWO VALVES PER CYLINDER
(32 VALVES IN ALL)
SIX-SPEED GEARBOX
OUTPUT: 418BHP AT 10,750RPM IN 1966

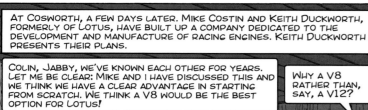

AT COSWORTH, A FEW DAYS LATER. MIKE COSTIN AND KEITH DUCKWORTH, FORMERLY OF LOTUS, HAVE BUILT UP A COMPANY DEDICATED TO THE DEVELOPMENT AND MANUFACTURE OF RACING ENGINES. KEITH DUCKWORTH PRESENTS THEIR PLANS.

COLIN, JABBY, WE'VE KNOWN EACH OTHER FOR YEARS. LET ME BE CLEAR: MIKE AND I HAVE DISCUSSED THIS AND WE THINK WE HAVE A CLEAR ADVANTAGE IN STARTING FROM SCRATCH. WE THINK A V8 WOULD BE THE BEST OPTION FOR LOTUS!

WHY A V8 RATHER THAN, SAY, A V12?

THE CLASSIC LAYOUT OF AN EIGHT-CYLINDER V-ENGINE ENSURES PLENTY OF POWER AND, ABOVE ALL, GOOD TORQUE OVER A BROAD RANGE.

A V8 OUGHT TO PLEASE FORD!

ANOTHER ADVANTAGE: A V8 IS LIGHT AND COMPACT.

VERY IMPORTANT!

AS FOR THE STANDARD 90° ANGLE, IT HELPS SMOOTHNESS AND RELIABILITY... AND, OF COURSE, TWIN OVERHEAD CAMSHAFTS AND FOUR VALVES PER CYLINDER PROVIDE STRONG POWER DELIVERY AT ALL ENGINE SPEEDS.

HOW MUCH POWER?

OUR DFV, OR DOUBLE FOUR-VALVE, SHOULD INITIALLY GIVE A LITTLE MORE THAN 400BHP AT 9,000RPM, WITH MAXIMUM TORQUE OF 370NM AT 7,000RPM.

SO, WE'RE NOT AIMING TO BE REVOLUTIONARY. OUR PRIMARY OBJECTIVE IS RELIABILITY BY USING TRIED AND TESTED TECHNOLOGY THAT IS FULLY UNDERSTOOD HERE AT COSWORTH!

I LIKE YOUR PLANS A LOT. WHAT WILL IT COST?

£100,000* TO BUILD AND RUN FIVE ENGINES FOR A YEAR.

*EQUIVALENT TO ABOUT £1.4 MILLION IN 2013.

FORD-COSWORTH V8:
CAPACITY: 2,993CC
BORE/STROKE: 85.72 x 64.83MM
DIRECT INJECTION
FOUR OHC, FOUR VALVES PER CYLINDER
(32 VALVES IN ALL)
FIVE-SPEED GEARBOX

FORD UK'S HQ AT WARLEY.

FORD WOULD BE THE IDEAL PARTNER TO ACHIEVE COSWORTH'S GOALS!

YES, WE USE FORD ENGINES IN OUR SEVEN AND THE ELAN. THE LOTUS CORTINA HAS BEEN A SUCCESS AND WE'RE WELL REGARDED BY FORD AFTER THE WIN AT INDIANAPOLIS...

WALTER, THE 'TOTAL PERFORMANCE' PROGRAMME IS TRANSFORMING FORD'S IMAGE RAPIDLY. WE HAVE SOMETHING HERE THAT WILL ENSURE FORD'S DOMINANCE IN F1!

INTERESTING. LET'S SEE IT!

BRIEFLY, THE FORD BRAND WILL BE FULLY ASSOCIATED WITH COSWORTH'S. THE SPIN-OFFS FOR YOU WILL BE HUGE. ALL FORD UK HAS TO DO IS TO AGREE TO INVEST £100,000 TO START DEVELOPMENT AND CONSTRUCTION OF THE ENGINE. I THINK YOU'LL ADMIT THAT IT'S NOT A FORTUNE!

WHILE WE'RE WAITING FOR THE DFV, WE'LL USE THE BRM H16 FOR THE START OF THE 1966 SEASON.

COLIN, YOUR PROPOSITION DOES INDEED LOOK VERY ATTRACTIVE. I'LL DO MY VERY BEST TO GET IT ACCEPTED BY FORD UK'S BOARD OF DIRECTORS.

BUT THE H16'S DEVELOPMENT IS BEHIND SCHEDULE AND IT ISN'T READY UNTIL MONZA.

WELL, THERE IT IS, AT LAST, THREE RACES FROM THE END OF THE SEASON!

BRM UNDER-ESTIMATED THE PROBLEMS OF SUCH A SET-UP. IT'S FAR FROM ACHIEVING THE EXPECTED POWER OUTPUT. AND THE ENGINE IS AS BIG AND HEAVY AS A HIPPOPOTAMUS: 260KG ON ITS OWN!

STILL, IT'LL BE BETTER THAN THE BORED-OUT CLIMAX WE'VE BEEN STRUGGLING WITH SINCE THE START OF THE SEASON!

LET'S SEE WHAT IT'S MADE OF.

38

BROOOO

ACCELERATION IS A LOT BETTER THAN THE 2-LITRE CLIMAX. THAT'S GOOD!

AND TOP SPEED IS FINE.

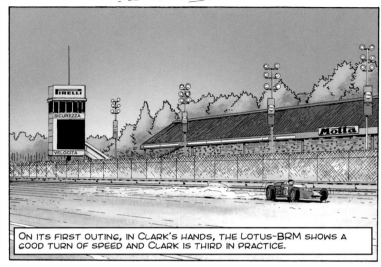

ON ITS FIRST OUTING, IN CLARK'S HANDS, THE LOTUS-BRM SHOWS A GOOD TURN OF SPEED AND CLARK IS THIRD IN PRACTICE.

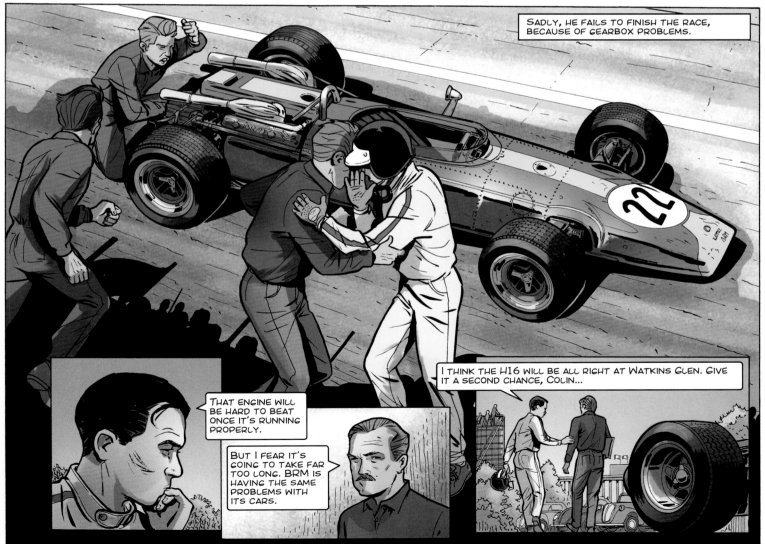

SADLY, HE FAILS TO FINISH THE RACE, BECAUSE OF GEARBOX PROBLEMS.

THAT ENGINE WILL BE HARD TO BEAT ONCE IT'S RUNNING PROPERLY.

BUT I FEAR IT'S GOING TO TAKE FAR TOO LONG. BRM IS HAVING THE SAME PROBLEMS WITH ITS CARS.

I THINK THE H16 WILL BE ALL RIGHT AT WATKINS GLEN. GIVE IT A SECOND CHANCE, COLIN...

RUNNING THE H16 ENGINE IN THE UNITED STATES GRAND PRIX IS A GAMBLE THAT PAYS OFF AS CLARK WINS THE RACE. IT IS TO BE THE ONLY F1 WIN FOR THE BRM H16 – SOMETHING OF A MIRACLE. MEANWHILE, THE AUSTRALIAN, JACK BRABHAM, IN HIS RATHER CRUDE BUT RELIABLE BRABHAM-REPCO, STRINGS TOGETHER A SERIES OF WINS AND TAKES THE DRIVERS' AND CONSTRUCTORS' CHAMPIONSHIPS. LOTUS, HOWEVER, IS A LONG WAY FROM REPEATING ITS SUCCESSES OF THE PREVIOUS SEASON.

EXCUSE ME, GRAHAM!

COLIN! AT LEAST YOU'VE MANAGED TO GET A WIN OUT OF THAT HEAP OF NUTS AND BOLTS. I HAVEN'T HAD SUCH LUCK THIS YEAR!

YES, I'M VERY KEEN TO USE THE FORD-COSWORTH ENGINE NEXT SEASON. I NEED TO SPEAK TO YOU ABOUT THAT...

THEY'RE OFFERING ME EXCLUSIVE USE OF THE V8 FOR 1967, BUT ONLY IF I CAN SIGN A SECOND DRIVER OF CLARK'S CALIBRE.

THEY'D LIKE... WELL, I'D LIKE... YOU TO RACE FOR LOTUS NEXT SEASON!

HILL AND CHAPMAN AGREE TO BURY THE HATCHET, BUT THE V8 STILL ISN'T READY!

COLIN, WHEN I AGREED TO LEAVE BRM, IT WASN'T TO FIND MYSELF STILL DRIVING THEIR H16!

I'M SORRY LADS! I THINK THIS WILL BE OUR LAST RACE WITH THE H16. FOR MONACO, WE'LL GO BACK TO THE 1966 SET-UP, WITH JIMMY IN THE CLIMAX V8 AND GRAHAM IN THE BRM V8. THE CARS WILL BE LESS POWERFUL, BUT LIGHT AND RELIABLE.

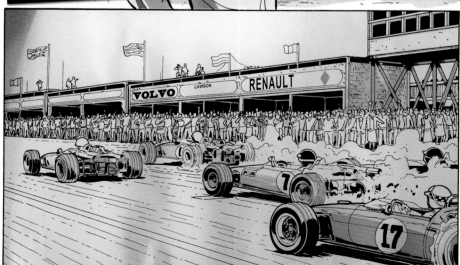

SOUTH AFRICA ENDS IN HILL RUNNING OFF THE TRACK AND CLARK RETIRING. AT MONACO, HILL FINISHES SECOND BUT CLARK SPINS OUT.

40

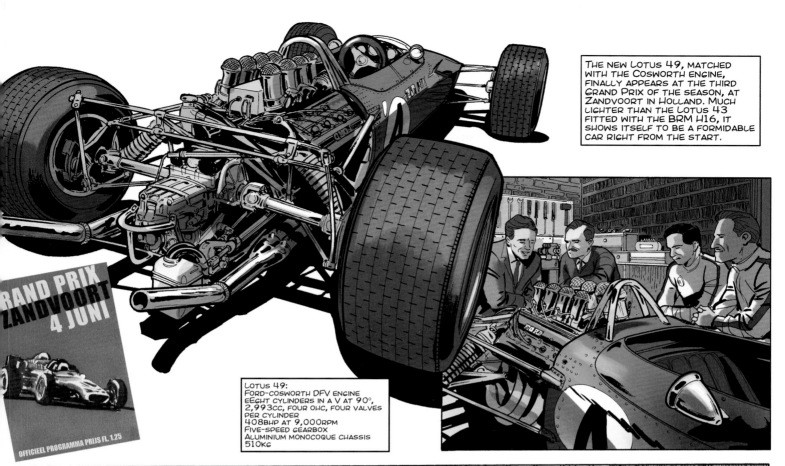

THE NEW LOTUS 49, MATCHED WITH THE COSWORTH ENGINE, FINALLY APPEARS AT THE THIRD GRAND PRIX OF THE SEASON, AT ZANDVOORT IN HOLLAND. MUCH LIGHTER THAN THE LOTUS 43 FITTED WITH THE BRM H16, IT SHOWS ITSELF TO BE A FORMIDABLE CAR RIGHT FROM THE START.

GRAND PRIX ZANDVOORT 4 JUNI

OFFICIEEL PROGRAMMA PRIJS FL. 1.25

LOTUS 49:
FORD-COSWORTH DFV ENGINE
EIGHT CYLINDERS IN A V AT 90°,
2,993CC, FOUR OHC, FOUR VALVES
PER CYLINDER
408BHP AT 9,000RPM
FIVE-SPEED GEARBOX
ALUMINIUM MONOCOQUE CHASSIS
510KG

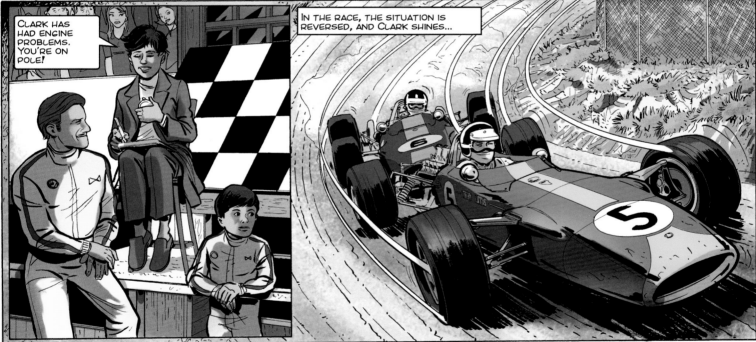

CLARK HAS HAD ENGINE PROBLEMS. YOU'RE ON POLE!

IN THE RACE, THE SITUATION IS REVERSED, AND CLARK SHINES...

...WHILE HILL CAN'T GET IN THE POINTS.

DAMN YOU, CHAPMAN!

THE 49'S FIRST RACE BRINGS POLE FOR HILL AND VICTORY FOR CLARK!

41

AFTER ZANDVOORT, EITHER CLARK OR HILL TAKES POLE IN THE NINE REMAINING RACES!

1M 25.3S! THIS ONE'S MINE!

I THINK WE HAVE THE ULTIMATE WEAPON HERE!

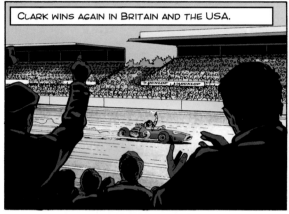

CLARK WINS AGAIN IN BRITAIN AND THE USA.

AT SPA, GURNEY WINS THE RACE WITH HIS EAGLE-WESLAKE.

THE LOTUS 49 LOOKS FEARSOME, BUT IT SUFFERS FROM TEETHING TROUBLES THAT TOO OFTEN MEAN VICTORY IS SURRENDERED TO THE SLOWER, BUT MORE RELIABLE, BRABHAM-REPCO CARS DRIVEN BY DENNY HULME AND JACK BRABHAM.

THE FINAL ROUND OF THE CHAMPIONSHIP IS PLAYED OUT IN MEXICO, BETWEEN THE BRABHAM-REPCO DRIVERS AND CLARK.

CLARK WINS THE GRAND PRIX, BUT HULME, THANKS TO HIS THIRD PLACE, TAKES THE DRIVERS' TITLE AND BRINGS BRABHAM-REPCO A FURTHER CONSTRUCTORS' TITLE. DESPITE HIS FOUR WINS, CLARK IS ONLY THIRD IN THE DRIVERS' CHAMPIONSHIP, WELL AHEAD OF HILL IN SEVENTH PLACE.

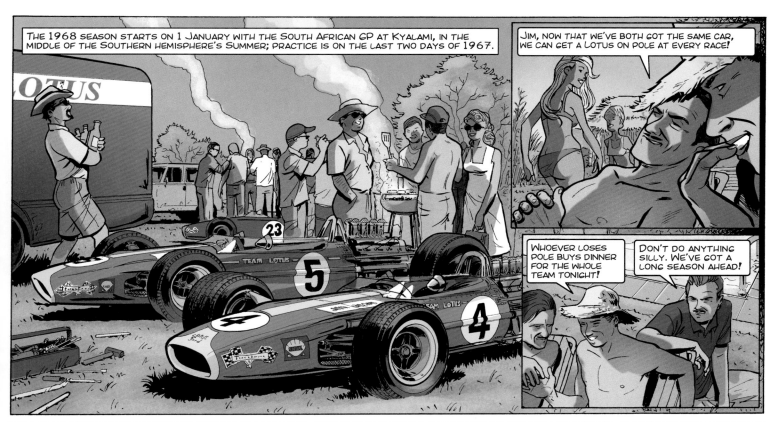

THE 1968 SEASON STARTS ON 1 JANUARY WITH THE SOUTH AFRICAN GP AT KYALAMI, IN THE MIDDLE OF THE SOUTHERN HEMISPHERE'S SUMMER; PRACTICE IS ON THE LAST TWO DAYS OF 1967.

JIM, NOW THAT WE'VE BOTH GOT THE SAME CAR, WE CAN GET A LOTUS ON POLE AT EVERY RACE!

WHOEVER LOSES POLE BUYS DINNER FOR THE WHOLE TEAM TONIGHT!

DON'T DO ANYTHING SILLY. WE'VE GOT A LONG SEASON AHEAD!

CLARK TAKES POLE POSITION, A FULL SECOND AHEAD OF HILL. IN THIRD POSITION IS JACKIE STEWART IN A MATRA MS9 'TEST CAR', USING THE FORD-COSWORTH ENGINE.

I'M LOOKING FORWARD TO A NICE IMPALA STEAK TONIGHT, GRAHAM!

STEWART'S MATRA SURPRISES EVERYONE AND IMMEDIATELY SURGES INTO THE LEAD.

BUT AFTER THE SECOND LAP, AT THE END OF THE LONG STRAIGHT, CLARK RECLAIMS HIS RIGHTFUL PLACE.

AFTER 80 LAPS, JIMMY SCORES HIS FIRST WIN OF THE YEAR. IT'S HIS 25TH IN ONLY 72 GRANDS PRIX, BEATING THE PREVIOUS RECORD SET IN 1957 BY THE GREAT JUAN MANUEL FANGIO.

43

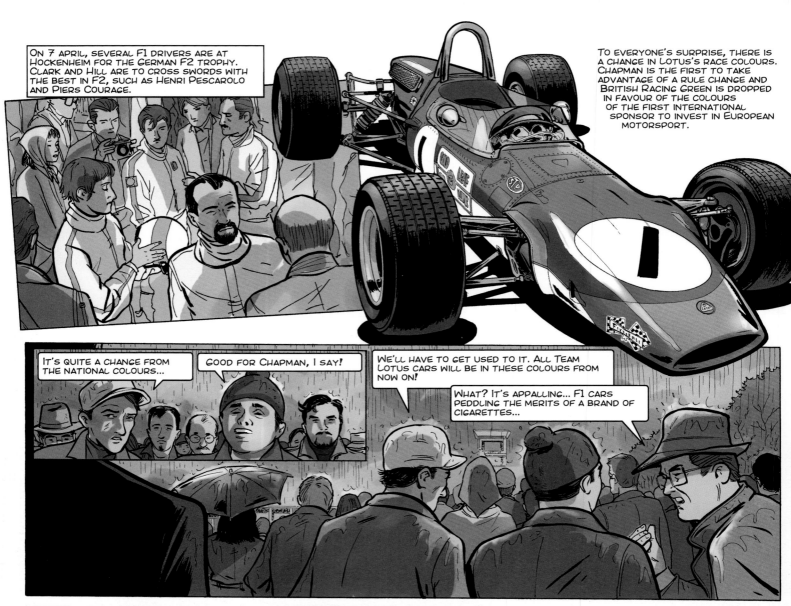

ON 7 APRIL, SEVERAL F1 DRIVERS ARE AT HOCKENHEIM FOR THE GERMAN F2 TROPHY. CLARK AND HILL ARE TO CROSS SWORDS WITH THE BEST IN F2, SUCH AS HENRI PESCAROLO AND PIERS COURAGE.

TO EVERYONE'S SURPRISE, THERE IS A CHANGE IN LOTUS'S RACE COLOURS. CHAPMAN IS THE FIRST TO TAKE ADVANTAGE OF A RULE CHANGE AND BRITISH RACING GREEN IS DROPPED IN FAVOUR OF THE COLOURS OF THE FIRST INTERNATIONAL SPONSOR TO INVEST IN EUROPEAN MOTORSPORT.

IT'S QUITE A CHANGE FROM THE NATIONAL COLOURS...

GOOD FOR CHAPMAN, I SAY!

WE'LL HAVE TO GET USED TO IT. ALL TEAM LOTUS CARS WILL BE IN THESE COLOURS FROM NOW ON!

WHAT? IT'S APPALLING... F1 CARS PEDDLING THE MERITS OF A BRAND OF CIGARETTES...

THE RACE HAS TWO HEATS. THE TRACK IS WET FOR THE FIRST HEAT AND BELTOISE AND PESCAROLO LEAD THE FIELD... THE LOTUSES AREN'T REALLY IN THEIR ELEMENT.

CLARK IS IN EIGHTH PLACE. SUDDENLY, ON THE THIRD LAP, AS HE'S ENTERING THE WOODED PART OF THE CIRCUIT...

44

THE CAR HIT THE TREES AT OVER 150MPH. LIKE SO MANY OF BOTH HIS FRIENDS AND RIVALS BEFORE HIM, JIMMY IS KILLED INSTANTLY. SEVERAL WEEKS LATER, THE ENQUIRY INSTIGATED BY CHAPMAN WOULD CONCLUDE THAT A SLOW PUNCTURE IN THE RIGHT REAR TYRE HAD CAUSED THE ACCIDENT.

THE TRAGIC NEWS SPREADS AROUND THE PADDOCK LIKE WILDFIRE. ALL THE DRIVERS ARE IN A STATE OF SHOCK.

45

GRAHAM HILL IN THE SECOND LOTUS PULLS OUT BEFORE THE SECOND HEAT.

HAS ANYONE GOT HOLD OF COLIN?

NOT YET. THEY CAN'T FIND HIM.

IT'S AWFUL... HE WAS SO YOUNG!

AND HE WAS EASILY THE BEST OF US... THE MOST TALENTED OF ALL THE DRIVERS. YET IT WASN'T ENOUGH TO SAVE HIM.

WHAT CAN WE LOOK FORWARD TO NOW?

CHAPMAN IS WITH HIS FAMILY, SKIING IN ST MORITZ.

Der alte Sultan

MR CHAPMAN!

MR CHAPMAN, I'M AFRAID I HAVE BAD NEWS FOR YOU.

WHAT'S THE MATTER...?

CHAPMAN DISAPPEARS WITHOUT TRACE FOR SEVERAL DAYS...

IT'S JIMMY.

OH MY GOD!

NOBODY – AT HOME, IN THE TEAM OR AT THE FACTORY – HAS ANY IDEA WHERE HE HAS GONE...

COME ON, WE'VE GOT TO GO...

46

APRIL 1968. A FEW DAYS AFTER THE TRAGIC DEATH OF JIM CLARK AT HOCKENHEIM.

COLIN CHAPMAN, STILL IN SHOCK AT THE LOSS OF HIS FRIEND AND LEADING DRIVER, SUMMONED THE STRENGTH TO CHARTER A SPECIAL PLANE TO ALLOW MEMBERS OF THE LOTUS TEAM TO ATTEND THE FUNERAL IN SCOTLAND. NUMEROUS DRIVERS ARE THERE. AROUND 1,100 PEOPLE TURN UP.

MOTOR RACING WAS NEVER A SPORT FOR THE FAINT-HEARTED. THE LIST OF F1 RACING DRIVERS WHO HAD LOST THEIR LIVES SINCE 1950 WAS NOTABLY LONG.

ONOFRE MARIMON.
EUGENIO CASTELLOTTI.
ARCHIE SCOTT BROWN.
LUIGI MUSSO.
PETER COLLINS.
STUART LEWIS-EVANS.
JEAN BEHRA.
IVOR BUEB.
HARRY SCHELL.
CHRIS BRISTOW.
ALAN STACEY.
WOLFGANG VON TRIPS.
RICARDO RODRIGUEZ.
CAREL GODIN DE BEAUFORT.
JOHN TAYLOR.
LORENZO BANDINI.
BOB ANDERSON...

BACK AT THE CHESHUNT WORKS, CHAPMAN SETS UP AN ENQUIRY.

LET ME BE QUITE CLEAR, PETER. I WANT TO KNOW EXACTLY WHAT CAUSED THIS CRASH AND JIMMY'S DEATH.

EVEN IF I BEAR SOME RESPONSIBILITY.

CHAPMAN CALLED UPON PETER JOWITT, AN ENGINEER SPECIALISING IN MILITARY AIRCRAFT ACCIDENTS AND ALSO AN RAC SCRUTINEER.

DO CONTACT CHRIS PARRY AT FIRESTONE, AS WELL AS KEITH DUCKWORTH OF COURSE. I WANT YOUR FINDINGS AS QUICKLY AS POSSIBLE...

A FEW WEEKS LATER, MIKE SPENCE IS TESTING A REVOLUTIONARY NEW LOTUS AT INDIANAPOLIS IN PREPARATION FOR THE INDY 500: THE 56 HAS FOUR-WHEEL DRIVE AND A 500BHP PRATT & WHITNEY GAS TURBINE ENGINE!

LOTUS 56:
500BHP PRATT & WHITNEY TURBINE
SINGLE SPEED
FOUR-WHEEL DRIVE
ALUMINIUM MONOCOQUE CHASSIS
610KG

LOTUS HAD ALREADY CAUSED A SENSATION AT INDIANAPOLIS IN 1963 WITH ITS REAR-ENGINED CAR.

CAUGHT OUT BY UNDERSTEER AND RUNNING WIDE, SPENCE SLIDES ALONG THE WALL AND IS HIT ON THE HEAD BY THE FRONT RIGHT WHEEL.

SCHRRRRRRRRRRRRRRRRRRRRR

A FEW HOURS LATER, SPENCE DIES FROM HIS INJURIES, JUST ONE MONTH TO THE DAY AFTER JIM CLARK'S DEATH.

WHEN CHAPMAN GETS THE NEWS, HE IS DEVASTATED AND DECIDES TO GIVE UP RACING. HE ASKS 'JABBY' CROMBAC TO SELL ALL THE EQUIPMENT AND PAY OFF THE BILLS.

BUT KNOWING COLIN WELL, CROMBAC DOES NOTHING.

DON'T WORRY, COLIN. I'LL TAKE CARE OF IT. YOU GO AND HAVE A FEW DAYS' REST...

THE SPANISH GP, MAY 1968. CHAPMAN STAYS AWAY.

IT LOOKS AS IF CHAPMAN MIGHT BE GIVING UP.

MAYBE... BUT IF LOTUS CARRIED ON, NOW THEY'RE WITHOUT CLARK, I DON'T THINK THEY'D WIN VERY OFTEN...

THE BRILLIANT TRIO OF LOTUS-CLARK-COSWORTH REIGNED SUPREME IN THE 1967 SEASON. BUT AFTER LOSING CLARK, TEAM LOTUS ALSO LOSES THE EXCLUSIVE DEAL WITH COSWORTH, WHO NOW ALSO SUPPLY MCLAREN, STEWART'S MATRA AND SIFFERT'S LOTUS.

JUST ONE WORKS LOTUS IS ENTERED, DRIVEN BY HILL. WITH THE CSI* HAVING OPENED THE DOOR TO SPONSORSHIP IN EARLY 1968, THE CAR CARRIES THE COLOURS OF THE FIRST NON-SPORTING SPONSOR IN F1.

LOTUS 49:
FORD COSWORTH DFV
90° V8 ENGINE, 2,993CC
FOUR VALVES PER CYLINDER
FOUR OHC, DIRECT INJECTION
408BHP AT 9,000RPM
FIVE-SPEED GEARBOX
ALUMINIUM MONOCOQUE CHASSIS,
510KG

* COMMISSION SPORTIVE INTERNATIONALE – THE PART OF THE FÉDÉRATION INTERNATIONALE DE L'AUTOMOBILE RESPONSIBLE FOR GOVERNING MOTORSPORT.

IT'S A GREAT OPPORTUNITY FOR TEAM LOTUS!

BELIEVE ME, SPONSORSHIP WILL SPEED UP THE DEVELOPMENT OF THE SPORT.

BUT SPONSORSHIP DOESN'T PLEASE EVERYONE.

I DON'T SMOKE... AND NOR DO MY CARS!

THE 1968 SEASON IS CERTAINLY NOT SHORT OF NEW DEVELOPMENTS. HAVING WON SEVERAL F3 AND F2 TITLES, MATRA MOVES INTO F1 WITH TWO CARS THAT MAKE USE OF AVIATION TECHNOLOGY.

MATRA INTERNATIONAL, RUN BY KEN TYRRELL, IS ENTERING THE MS10-COSWORTH. IT'LL BE DRIVEN BY JACKIE STEWART AS SOON AS HE'S REGAINED THE USE OF THE WRIST HE DISLOCATED IN F2...

DIRECTED BY JEAN-LUC LAGARDÈRE, THE FRENCH COMPANY DESIGNS AND BUILDS MISSILES AND SPORTS CARS.

THE MS11, WITH A MATRA V12 ENGINE, AND ENTERED BY MATRA SPORT, WILL BE DRIVEN BY JEAN-PIERRE BELTOISE AT THE MONACO GRAND PRIX.

NO EXPENSE SPARED!

TRUE, BUT IT'S ODD TO HAVE INVESTED IN TWO DIFFERENT CARS...

BELTOISE IN THE MATRA MS11-COSWORTH AND CHRIS AMON IN THE FERRARI 312 ALTERNATELY LEAD THE RACE, BEFORE ENCOUNTERING MECHANICAL PROBLEMS.

ROOAAAU ROOAAAAA

IN THE END IT'S HILL WHO WINS THE SPANISH GP AND TAKES THE LEAD IN THE CHAMPIONSHIP.

GRAHAM'S DETERMINATION IMPRESSES EVERYONE IN THE TEAM, STILL REELING FROM THE DEATHS OF CLARK AND SPENCE.

SUPERB, GRAHAM!

A BRILLIANT RACE!

LOOK OVER THERE! IT'S CHAPMAN!

HE'S CLEARLY BACK...

26e grand prix automobile de monaco

CHAPMAN IS BACK IN BUSINESS WITH A VENGEANCE! THE LOTUS, NOW DESIGNATED 49B, IS NEWLY FITTED WITH FRONT AEROFOILS AND A REAR SPOILER.

AEROFOILS WERE FIRST DEVELOPED IN THE EARLY 1950s BY PORSCHE AND MERCEDES BEFORE REAPPEARING IN 1966 WHEN CHAPARRAL UNVEILED THE 2E FOR THE CAN-AM*. ITS HUGE MOVEABLE AEROFOIL ENHANCED DRIVEABILITY, ROAD-HOLDING AND BRAKING.

* THE CAN-AM SERIES, HELD IN CANADA AND THE USA, BEGAN IN 1966 AND SAW VERY POWERFUL SPORTS CARS BATTLING IT OUT, THANKS TO UNLIMITED ENGINE CAPACITY.

INTRIGUED, CHAPMAN MANAGED TO RECORD DATA ON THE LOTUS 38's AERODYNAMIC LIFT USING AN AIRCRAFT BLACK BOX IN MAY 1967 DURING CLARK'S QUALIFYING RUNS AT INDIANAPOLIS.

COLIN IS WELL AWARE OF THE INTEREST AEROFOILS WILL AROUSE.

THE THING IS, JABBY, THE AEROFOILS SHOULD GENERATE SEVERAL HUNDRED POUNDS OF DOWNFORCE.

DOWNFORCE

LIFT

DOWNFORCE

THIS WILL COUNTERACT THE AERODYNAMIC LIFT CREATED BY THE MOVEMENT OF THE CAR THROUGH THE AIR.

CHAPMAN ENTERS A SECOND CAR AT MONACO FOR THE YOUNG JACKIE OLIVER, A FORMER LOTUS F2 DRIVER. NEW TO THE CIRCUIT, HE MANAGES ONLY 13TH PLACE ON THE GRID.

WELL DONE ON GETTING POLE, GRAHAM!

SUNDAY 26 MAY 1968. THE START OF THE MONACO GRAND PRIX.

JOHNNY SERVOZ-GAVIN MAKES A FINE START IN HIS MATRA MS10...

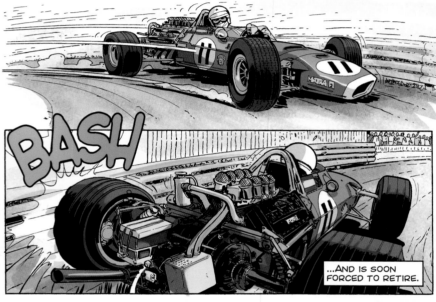

...BUT HE IS TOO AGGRESSIVE...

BASH

...AND IS SOON FORCED TO RETIRE.

HILL SUPERBLY WINS HIS FOURTH MONACO GP!

GRAHAM, I BOW TO YOUR TALENT!

I'M FLATTERED TO HEAR IT FROM YOU...

AND WE'RE NICELY AHEAD IN THE CHAMPIONSHIP!

BUT NOT EVERYONE MERITS COLIN'S CONGRATULATIONS.

JACKIE, I WARNED YOU THAT THE MONACO GP IS A RACE OF ATTRITION...

BUT SCARFIOTTI AND MCLAREN COLLIDED JUST IN FRONT OF ME...

THAT'S WHAT I MEANT! YOU NEED TO WATCH OUT, LAD...

YOU'RE NOT FOCUSED ENOUGH...

FOUR DAYS AFTER THE MONACO GP IT'S THE INDIANAPOLIS 500. THREE LOTUS 56s ARE ENTERED. JOE LEONARD TAKES POLE AHEAD OF GRAHAM HILL, WHILE ART POLLARD IS IN FOURTH POSITION.

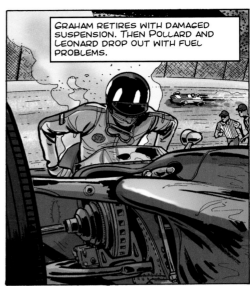

GRAHAM RETIRES WITH DAMAGED SUSPENSION. THEN POLLARD AND LEONARD DROP OUT WITH FUEL PROBLEMS.

VICTORY EVENTUALLY GOES TO BOBBY UNSER IN HIS EAGLE-OFFENHAUSER.

USAC* HAS REFUSED TO BAN REAR-ENGINED CARS, BUT MARK MY WORDS, THIS TURBINE SAGA HAS GONE ON LONG ENOUGH!

YOU BET! THESE AREN'T AIRPLANES WE'RE RACING...

...AND TURBINES WERE DULY BANNED THE FOLLOWING SEASON.

*UNITED STATES AUTOMOBILE CLUB – THE GOVERNING BODY OF INDYCAR RACING

BY THE BELGIAN GP, LOTUS HAS BEEN COPIED: THE FERRARIS AND BRABHAMS HAVE AEROFOILS.

AT THE END OF A RACE PACKED WITH RETIREMENTS, BRUCE MCLAREN TOOK VICTORY, HIS TEAM'S FIRST IN F1.

AT LOTUS, COLIN WAS LOOKING GRIM.

WHY THE DEVIL HAS THIS UJ COME LOOSE?

AND OLIVER'S FIFTH PLACE DIDN'T MAKE HIM FEEL ANY BETTER.

AS FOR YOU, JACKIE, PLEASE DON'T TELL ME THAT IT FEELS GREAT TO COME IN TWO LAPS BEHIND THE WINNER!

COLIN, HE'S INEXPERIENCED. BETTER TO GIVE HIM SOME HELPFUL ADVICE AND A CAR CAPABLE OF LASTING THE RACE!

AT ZANDVOORT, STEWART BRINGS MATRA ITS FIRST F1 WIN. AND BELTOISE MAKES IT A ONE-TWO IN THE MS11.

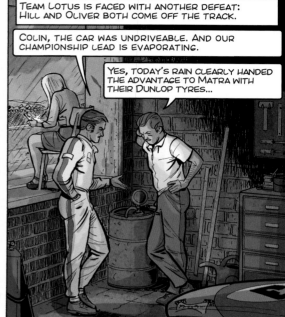

TEAM LOTUS IS FACED WITH ANOTHER DEFEAT: HILL AND OLIVER BOTH COME OFF THE TRACK.

COLIN, THE CAR WAS UNDRIVEABLE. AND OUR CHAMPIONSHIP LEAD IS EVAPORATING.

YES, TODAY'S RAIN CLEARLY HANDED THE ADVANTAGE TO MATRA WITH THEIR DUNLOP TYRES...

7 JULY 1968.

ROUEN-LES ESSARTS IS KNOWN AS 'A MAN'S CIRCUIT'!

ALL THE DRIVERS LIKE THE FAST STRETCHES, ESPECIALLY THE SWOOP DOWN TO THE FAMOUS HAIRPIN.

WITH AEROFOILS, IT'S AN UPHILL TASK FOR HILL AND OLIVER. THEY QUALIFY SOME WAY BEHIND RINDT, THE POLESITTER.

WE'RE GOING TO HAVE TO ADJUST THE REAR AEROFOIL. THE FRONT WHEELS ARE GOING LIGHT IN SOME PLACES.

THE GENIAL FRENCHMAN, JO SCHLESSER, IS MAKING HIS F1 DEBUT AT THE AGE OF 40 IN THE BRAND-NEW RA302, BUILT PARTIALLY FROM MAGNESIUM. SURTEES REFUSES TO DRIVE IT, FINDING IT IMPOSSIBLE TO HANDLE.

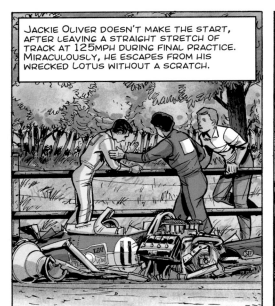

Jackie Oliver doesn't make the start, after leaving a straight stretch of track at 125mph during final practice. Miraculously, he escapes from his wrecked Lotus without a scratch.

Shortly before the start, all the drivers ride around the track in Matra 530 road cars, greeting the large crowd.

The weather is overcast and threatening. Jacky Ickx has his Ferrari fitted with rain tyres.

From the start, Stewart leads, closely followed by Rindt and Ickx.

But at the end of the first lap, the first drops of rain start falling and Ickx moves into the lead.

ON THE THIRD LAP, SCHLESSER LOSES CONTROL OF THE HONDA ON A BEND AND CLIPS THE BANK.

THE CAR IMMEDIATELY CATCHES FIRE AND THE HIGHLY FLAMMABLE MAGNESIUM OF THE CHASSIS INTENSIFIES THE FLAMES.

DESPITE THE FIREFIGHTERS' INTERVENTION, SCHLESSER IS TRAPPED IN THE CAR AND SADLY PERISHES. YET THE RACE CONTINUES. FOLLOWING CLARK, SPENCE AND SCARFIOTTI, HE IS THE FOURTH DRIVER TO BE KILLED SINCE THE START OF THE 1968 SEASON.

WITH A VIOLENT DOWNPOUR POUNDING THE TRACK, YOUNG JACKY ICKX'S FERRARI, ON RAIN TYRES, BUILDS UP A LEAD OVER PEDRO RODRIGUEZ AND JOHN SURTEES.

AT QUARTER-DISTANCE, HILL, IN FOURTH PLACE, RETIRES FOR THE THIRD RACE RUNNING, WITH A BROKEN DRIVESHAFT...

A FEW MINUTES LATER, JO SIFFERT PULLS UP BESIDE HIM...

IT'S OK, NOTHING SERIOUS.

DAMN IT GRAHAM, I CAN'T SEE A THING THROUGH MY VISOR!

HERE, TAKE MINE. HANG ON A SEC...

THANKS!

ICKX FINALLY CLAIMS VICTORY AFTER A RACE LASTING TWO HOURS 25 MINUTES.

IT'S ICKX'S FIRST F1 WIN. FERRARI HADN'T WON SINCE MONZA IN 1966.

AT TEAM LOTUS, THERE ARE LONG FACES ALL ROUND. CHAPMAN IS GOING TO HAVE TO SOLVE THE BROKEN DRIVESHAFT PROBLEM QUICKLY.

COLIN, WE SEEM TO HAVE GONE BACK TO 1959. YOU'VE GOT TO GET THIS DRIVESHAFT PROBLEM SORTED OUT!

I HAVE TO FINISH THE NEXT RACE. I'M ONLY EIGHT POINTS CLEAR OF STEWART AND ICKX!

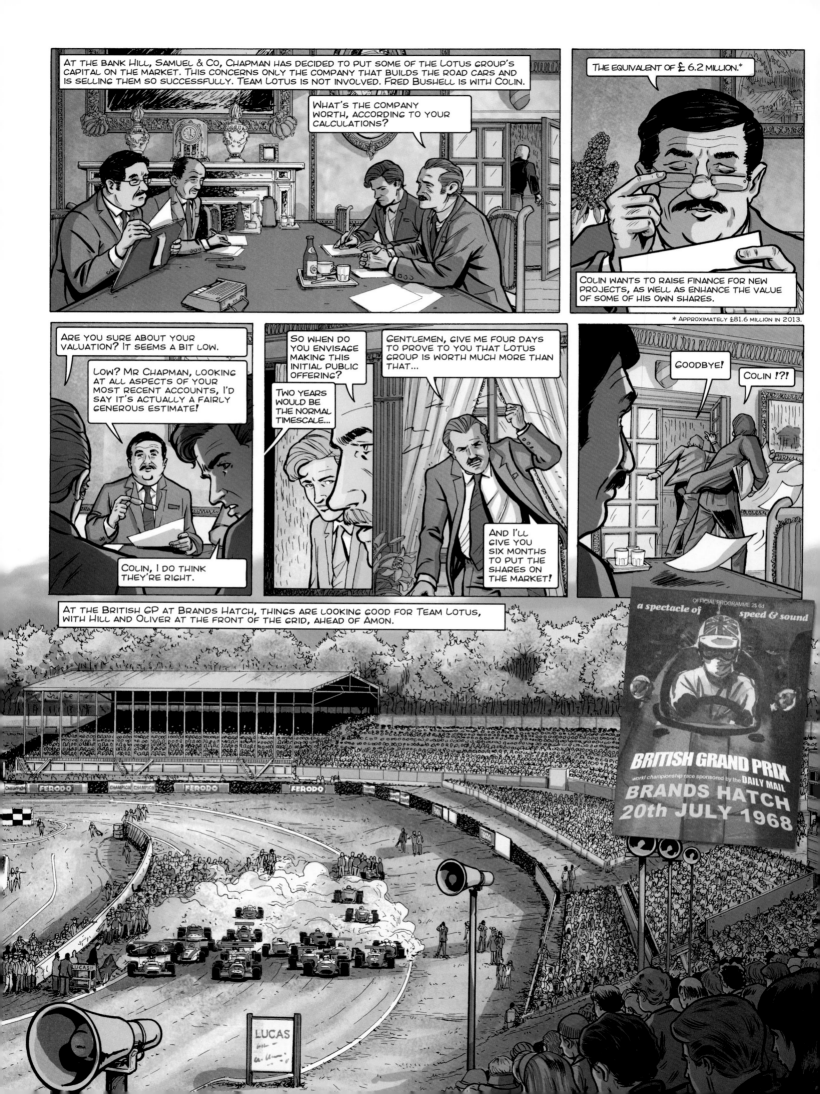

AT THE BANK HILL, SAMUEL & CO, CHAPMAN HAS DECIDED TO PUT SOME OF THE LOTUS GROUP'S CAPITAL ON THE MARKET. THIS CONCERNS ONLY THE COMPANY THAT BUILDS THE ROAD CARS AND IS SELLING THEM SO SUCCESSFULLY. TEAM LOTUS IS NOT INVOLVED. FRED BUSHELL IS WITH COLIN.

WHAT'S THE COMPANY WORTH, ACCORDING TO YOUR CALCULATIONS?

THE EQUIVALENT OF £ 6.2 MILLION.*

COLIN WANTS TO RAISE FINANCE FOR NEW PROJECTS, AS WELL AS ENHANCE THE VALUE OF SOME OF HIS OWN SHARES.

* APPROXIMATELY £81.6 MILLION IN 2013.

ARE YOU SURE ABOUT YOUR VALUATION? IT SEEMS A BIT LOW.

LOW? MR CHAPMAN, LOOKING AT ALL ASPECTS OF YOUR MOST RECENT ACCOUNTS, I'D SAY IT'S ACTUALLY A FAIRLY GENEROUS ESTIMATE!

COLIN, I DO THINK THEY'RE RIGHT.

SO WHEN DO YOU ENVISAGE MAKING THIS INITIAL PUBLIC OFFERING?

TWO YEARS WOULD BE THE NORMAL TIMESCALE...

GENTLEMEN, GIVE ME FOUR DAYS TO PROVE TO YOU THAT LOTUS GROUP IS WORTH MUCH MORE THAN THAT...

AND I'LL GIVE YOU SIX MONTHS TO PUT THE SHARES ON THE MARKET!

GOODBYE!

COLIN !?!

AT THE BRITISH GP AT BRANDS HATCH, THINGS ARE LOOKING GOOD FOR TEAM LOTUS, WITH HILL AND OLIVER AT THE FRONT OF THE GRID, AHEAD OF AMON.

OFFICIAL PROGRAMME 2s. 6d

a spectacle of   speed & sound

BRITISH GRAND PRIX
world championship race sponsored by the DAILY MAIL
BRANDS HATCH
20th JULY 1968

AFTER THREE LAPS, THREE LOTUSES ARE LEADING THE FIELD: OLIVER AHEAD OF HILL AND SIFFERT, WHO'S DRIVING THE BRAND-NEW 49B ENTERED BY ROB WALKER.

DUNLOP

OLIVER HAS REALLY STARTED THE RACE WELL. THAT'S GREAT PROGRESS!

YES... NOT BAD.

GRAHAM HILL HAS JUST STOPPED HIS CAR AT THE TRACKSIDE!

DAMN!

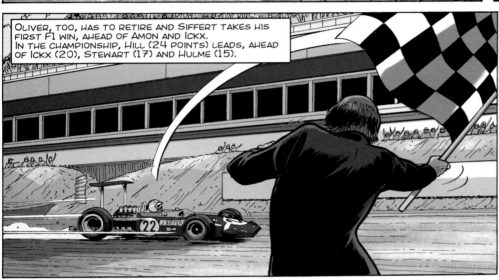

OLIVER, TOO, HAS TO RETIRE AND SIFFERT TAKES HIS FIRST F1 WIN, AHEAD OF AMON AND ICKX. IN THE CHAMPIONSHIP, HILL (24 POINTS) LEADS, AHEAD OF ICKX (20), STEWART (17) AND HULME (15).

WELL DONE, ROB! BY THE WAY, DID YOU FIT DIFFERENT DRIVESHAFTS FROM THOSE WE SUPPLIED?

NO, NOT AT ALL.

IT'S ALMOST AS IF SOMEONE HAS PUT A CURSE ON OUR TRANSMISSIONS!

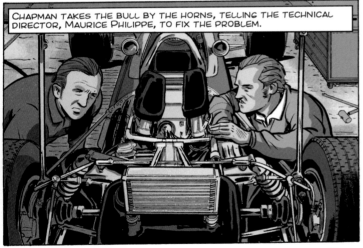

CHAPMAN TAKES THE BULL BY THE HORNS, TELLING THE TECHNICAL DIRECTOR, MAURICE PHILIPPE, TO FIX THE PROBLEM.

I THINK THE CAUSE IS THE EXTRA STRESS ON THE TRANSMISSION GENERATED BY THE REAR AEROFOIL...

WHATEVER IT IS, MAURICE, FIND ANOTHER SUPPLIER QUICKLY! IT WOULD BE RIDICULOUS TO LOSE THE CHAMPIONSHIP BECAUSE OF THAT...

AFTER A HELLISH GERMAN GP, HILL FINISHES SECOND TO STEWART.

MONZA SEES ANOTHER RETIREMENT. THE WINNERS ARE NEVER THE SAME FROM ONE RACE TO THE NEXT. HILL STILL HAS A SLENDER LEAD IN THE CHAMPIONSHIP OVER ICKX, STEWART AND HULME.

13

WHAT DO THINK OF ANDRETTI AND RINDT?

THEY'RE BIG NAMES AND THEY'RE BOTH YOUNG. JOCHEN HAS BEEN A FRONT-RUNNER ALL SEASON, DESPITE HIS BRABHAM-REPCO BEING RATHER UNDERPOWERED...

MARIO IS 28 AND HAS WON ALMOST EVERYTHING IN THE USA.

YES, I REALLY RATE HIM.

THE UNITED STATES GP AT WATKINS GLEN. TEAM LOTUS ENTERS A THIRD LOTUS 49B FOR ANDRETTI.

WHAT DO THINK OF THE CAR'S SET-UP, MARIO?

IT'S JUST RIGHT. I'LL BE ON POLE TOMORROW!

LET'S NOT OVERDO IT, I'M NOT ASKING THAT MUCH FIRST TIME!

DURING PRACTICE...

HOW DOES IT LOOK?

MARIO, GRAHAM AND STEWART ARE WITHIN A TENTH OF A SECOND OF EACH OTHER. WE'LL HAVE TO WAIT FOR THE OFFICIAL RESULTS.

ANDRETTI IS IN POLE POSITION, 0.07SEC AHEAD OF STEWART AND 0.08SEC AHEAD OF HILL!

INCREDIBLE!

AT THE END, STEWART WINS FROM HILL AND SURTEES.

YOU'RE LEADING THE CHAMPIONSHIP WITH 39 POINTS; STEWART HAS 36 AND HULME 33...

BLIMEY! IT'S GOING TO BE HOT IN MEXICO!

SO THERE ARE THREE DRIVERS WHO COULD TAKE THE TITLE IN THIS FINAL GRAND PRIX OF THE SEASON: HILL IS THIRD ON THE GRID, HULME FOURTH AND STEWART SEVENTH.

VII GRAN PREMIO MEXICO
DOMINGO 3 DE NOVEMBRE 1968

SIFFERT MESSES UP HIS START AND HILL TAKES THE LEAD AHEAD OF SURTEES, WHO SURGES UP FROM THE THIRD ROW!

VROAAA WROAAA A WRAAAAWWW

A FEW LAPS LATER, STEWART IS RIGHT ON HILL'S TAIL.

WHAT AN INCREDIBLE BATTLE IT IS BETWEEN THESE TWO FANTASTIC DRIVERS...

JUST AS GRAHAM AGAIN TAKES THE LEAD FROM THE SCOTSMAN...

I'M HEARING THAT HULME HAS RETIRED. SO NOW TWO DRIVERS ARE IN CONTENTION FOR THE TITLE!

HULME OUT 1:54

SUDDENLY, SOMETHING VERY STRANGE HAPPENS. A DOG IS STANDING IN THE MIDDLE OF THE TRACK!

HILL JUST MISSES IT...

BUT STEWART DOESN'T SEE THE DOG UNTIL THE LAST MOMENT AND HITS IT. HE HAS TO MAKE A PIT STOP.

STEWART'S MECHANICS QUICKLY CHANGE THE CAR'S NOSECONE AND A FRONT WHEEL. WHAT AN INCREDIBLE STROKE OF FATE...

STEWART GETS AWAY AGAIN, BUT IS NOW A LAP BEHIND GRAHAM HILL.

WRAAAAA

HILL WINS THE RACE AND HIS SECOND DRIVERS' WORLD CHAMPIONSHIP!

AND OUR OWN PEDRO RODRIGUEZ FINISHES A SUPERB FOURTH!

WHAT A RACE! GOODBYE FROM ME, RRRAMON RRRAMIREZ, AND BACK TO THE STUDIO...

TEAM LOTUS TAKES ITS THIRD CONSTRUCTORS' CHAMPIONSHIP AHEAD OF MCLAREN AND MATRA. AND FORD HAS ITS 15TH WIN AND THE UNOFFICIAL TITLE OF BEST ENGINE MANUFACTURER.

WELL DONE, GRAHAM!

I THINK FATE WAS ON OUR SIDE TODAY!

DESPITE HAVING FINISHED IN A SPLENDID THIRD PLACE, JACKIE OLIVER REALISES THAT HE WON'T BE A TEAM LOTUS DRIVER NEXT SEASON.

KEN TYRRELL AND COLIN CHAPMAN TAKE ADVANTAGE OF THEIR TRIP TO MEXICO TO VISIT THE AZTEC PYRAMIDS, WITH THEIR WIVES AND JABBY CROMBAC.

YOU KNOW, COLIN, I ENVY YOUR BUSINESS SKILLS!

CHAPMAN HAS FINALLY PERSUADED THE BANKERS TO VALUE HIS COMPANY AT £8.6 MILLION*, 26 TIMES THE ANNUAL PROFITS. ALL THE SHARES HAVE FOUND BUYERS AND COLIN HAS POCKETED £3.4 MILLION**, WHILE RETAINING 52% OF THE CAPITAL!

SO YOU'RE A MULTI-MILLIONAIRE NOW!

IT'S JUST PAPER, KEN, JUST PAPER!

* APPROXIMATELY £92.5 MILLION IN 2013. ** APPROXIMATELY £37 MILLION IN 2013.

17

CHRISTMAS 1968. COLIN AND HAZEL'S CHILDREN HAVE GROWN: JANE IS 12, SARAH 10 AND CLIVE 6.

WELL, CLIVE, WHAT DID FATHER CHRISTMAS BRING YOU?

LOOK, DADDY, IT'S JIMMY'S LOTUS! IT'S JUST WHAT I WANTED!

THIS WILL BE OUR LAST CHRISTMAS HERE. NEXT YEAR WE'LL BE CELEBRATING IN OUR NEW HOME AT EAST CARLETON.

I HOPE YOU'LL BE ABLE TO DEVOTE A LITTLE MORE TIME TO THE CHILDREN NOW...

I HOPE SO TOO, BUT WE REALLY HAVE TO MAKE THE PROFIT WE PROMISED OUR SHAREHOLDERS...

YOU'RE INCORRIGIBLE!

COLIN HAS PUT PRESSURE ON GRAHAM ARNOLD, SALES DIRECTOR FOR THE PRODUCTION CARS.

SO, ARNOLD, HOW ARE SALES GOING?

IT'S NOT EASY! OUR TARGETS ARE VERY HIGH.

IN 1969, THE LOTUS RANGE COMPRISES THREE MODELS.

LOTUS ELAN +2:
FORD LOTUS TWIN-CAM ENGINE, FRONT-MOUNTED
FOUR CYLINDERS IN LINE, 1,558CC
115BHP AT 6,000RPM
FOUR-SPEED GEARBOX,
REAR-WHEEL DRIVE
GIRDER CHASSIS
GLASS-FIBRE BODY

AVERAGE ANNUAL SALES ARE 1,300 FOR THE EUROPA, 700 FOR THE ELAN +2 AND 500 FOR THE ELAN.

LOTUS ELAN S3:
FORD LOTUS TWIN-CAM ENGINE, FRONT-MOUNTED
FOUR CYLINDERS IN LINE, 1,558CC
115BHP AT 6,000RPM
FOUR-SPEED GEARBOX, GIRDER CHASSIS
GLASS-FIBRE BODY

BUT I SHOULD MANAGE IT...

I'M RELYING ON YOU!

LOTUS EUROPA S2:
RENAULT ENGINE, MID-MOUNTED
FOUR CYLINDERS IN LINE, 1,470CC
78BHP AT 6,000RPM
FOUR-SPEED GEARBOX, REAR-WHEEL DRIVE, GIRDER CHASSIS
GLASS-FIBRE BODY
620KG

1969

CHAPMAN HIRES TONY RUDD TO OVERSEE THE PRODUCTION OF ROAD CARS AND TO DEVELOP THE PLANNED LOTUS ENGINE.

IT'S GOOD TO HAVE YOU HERE!

I'M PLEASED TO COME TO LOTUS — KEEN TO GET DOWN TO WORK!

THE LOTUS ENGINE WILL GRADUALLY BE FITTED TO ALL THE ROAD CARS.

LET'S START OFF WITH A LOOK AT OUR ASSEMBLY LINE.

AS YOU CAN SEE, ALL OUR CARS ARE BUILT AROUND A BACKBONE CHASSIS...

WITH THE 1969 SEASON COMING UP, A NUMBER OF DRIVERS HAVE CHANGED TEAMS. CHAPMAN, AT CONSIDERABLE EXPENSE, HAS MANAGED TO POACH JOCHEN RINDT, THE AUSTRIAN DRIVER, FROM THE BRABHAM TEAM, WHERE ICKX WILL TAKE HIS PLACE.

RIGHT, JOCHEN, LET'S GET TO WORK. I'M PAYING YOU ENOUGH!

THAT'S NOT THE COLIN I KNOW...

JIMMY'S DEATH REALLY AFFECTED HIM. HE'S DECIDED NOT TO GET TOO CLOSE TO HIS DRIVERS.

THE SOUTH AFRICAN GP – MARCH 1969. AT MATRA, THE OVERWEIGHT V12 HAS BEEN DITCHED AND LAGARDÈRE HAS DECIDED TO CONCENTRATE HIS EFFORTS ON TYRRELL'S TEAM: STEWART AND BELTOISE WILL DRIVE THE MS10.

THE ENTRY LIST IS MUCH SHORTER. FERRARI HAS JUST SOLD 50% OF ITS SHARES TO FIAT AND THE SCUDERIA IS IN THE MIDDLE OF RESTRUCTURING. CHRIS AMON IS THE ONLY DRIVER AND HAS TWO CARS AT HIS DISPOSAL. WITH HONDA AND COOPER HAVING PULLED OUT, SURTEES AND OLIVER HAVE JOINED BRM.

AEROFOILS ARE BIGGER, HIGHER AND MORE NUMEROUS THAN EVER. BRABHAM HAS MOVED IN WITH THE COSWORTH FAMILY. TWELVE CARS OUT OF 18 HAVE V8 ENGINES. ONLY FERRARI AND BRM, WITH THEIR V12s, ARE HOLDING OUT AGAINST THE TIDE.

STEWART WINS THE FIRST RACE FROM HILL. RINDT HAS TO RETIRE WITH FUEL PROBLEMS.

SPURRED ON BY JO BONNIER AND JACKIE STEWART, THE GPDA* ACTIVELY LOBBIES IN FAVOUR OF GREATER SAFETY FOR DRIVERS AND SPECTATORS.

* GRAND PRIX DRIVERS' ASSOCIATION, SET UP IN 1961.

MORE AND MORE DRIVERS ARE DYING IN FIRES.

LOOK WHAT HAPPENED TO BANDINI AND SCHLESSER, NOT TO MENTION BIANCHI A FEW WEEKS AGO AT LE MANS!

WHAT ABOUT PESCAROLO? A MIRACULOUS ESCAPE*.

*HENRI PESCAROLO ALSO CRASHED AT LE MANS, IN HIS MATRA 640 ON THE HUNAUDIÈRES STRAIGHT, ON 16 APRIL 1969.

THE GRAND PRIX DRIVERS' ASSOCIATION MEETS SEVERAL TIMES A YEAR, AND HAS MANAGED TO GET FIREPROOF CLOTHING MADE MANDATORY; SEAT BELTS REMAINED ONLY A RECOMMENDATION IN 1969...

I'M GOING BACK ON THE ATTACK WITH THE FIA*...

*FÉDÉRATION INTERNATIONALE DE L'AUTOMOBILE – THE GOVERNING BODY OF MOTORSPORT WORLDWIDE.

ASK THEM TO WORK ON FUEL TANKS AND HOSES. IT CAN'T GO ON LIKE THIS!

SO WHO'S GOING TO INSPECT THE TRACK AT SPA?

I AM. I'M GOING IN A FEW DAYS... AND WE'LL COME BACK TO AEROFOILS AT OUR NEXT MEETING.

THE SECOND GP OF THE SEASON TAKES PLACE IN SPAIN, AT THE MAGNIFICENT MONTJUÏC PARK ON THE OUTSKIRTS OF BARCELONA. IT'S A HILLY CIRCUIT AND THERE ARE SOME FAST BENDS.

VROOOAa

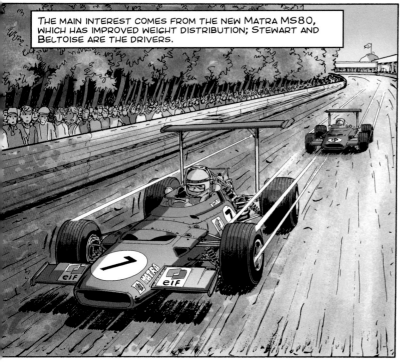

THE MAIN INTEREST COMES FROM THE NEW MATRA MS80, WHICH HAS IMPROVED WEIGHT DISTRIBUTION; STEWART AND BELTOISE ARE THE DRIVERS.

IN THE EARLY STAGES, RINDT OPENS UP A LEAD. HILL IS IN THIRD PLACE, HELD UP BY AMON UNTIL THE FERRARI'S ENGINE GIVES OUT.

JUST PAST THE PITS, THE CARS BECOME AIRBORNE AFTER HITTING A HUMP ON A FAST LEFT-HAND BEND.

SUDDENLY, ON THE NINTH LAP...

THE DAMNED AEROFOIL FOLDED LIKE PAPER. I WAS DOING 135MPH!

WE'VE GOT TO WARN JOCHEN! THE SAME COULD HAPPEN TO HIM...

21

ON THE 20TH LAP...

THIS TIME, IT'S THE TWO ENDS OF THE AEROFOIL AND ITS TWO SUPPORTS THAT BUCKLE AS THE CAR CLEARS THE HUMP. THE CAR TAKES OFF AND THEN CLIPS THE BARRIER.

JOCHEN IS TRAPPED IN HIS CAR.

FORTUNATELY, THE MARSHALS ARE QUICKLY ON THE SPOT.

RINDT IS TAKEN TO HOSPITAL. ONLY A FEW DAYS BEFORE THE RACE, HE HAD INSISTED THAT THE ORGANISERS INSTALL GUARDRAILS ALONG THIS PART OF THE TRACK.

THE GRAND PRIX ENDS WITH A WIN FOR STEWART, AHEAD OF MCLAREN AND BELTOISE.

DRIVER SAFETY IS NOW AN EVEN BIGGER PRIORITY FOR THE GPDA!

22

RINDT HAS A BROKEN NOSE AND A SKULL FRACTURE. A FEW DAYS LATER, WITH THE HELP OF HIS MANAGER, BERNIE ECCLESTONE, HE WRITES AN OPEN LETTER TO THE PRESS, QUESTIONING THE USE OF AEROFOILS.

THIS IS HOW I WANT IT TO START: "THIS IS AN OPEN LETTER TO EVERYONE WITH AN INTEREST IN FORMULA 1 RACING."

FOR SOME WEEKS, THE DIALOGUE BETWEEN CHAPMAN AND RINDT TAKES PLACE VIA CROMBAC AND ECCLESTONE!

JABBY, THIS MAN'S COMPLETELY MAD... HE WANTS TO KILL OFF ONE OF THE BEST INVENTIONS IN MOTORSPORT...

LISTEN TO THIS: "...AEROFOILS ARE DANGEROUS, MAINLY FOR THE DRIVERS, BUT ALSO FOR THE SPECTATORS."

IT LOOKS AS IF YOU'LL SOON HAVE A SHOWDOWN OVER YOUR GAMBLE...

AT THE MONACO GP, DESPITE THE CARS HAVING USED AEROFOILS IN THE FIRST PRACTICE SESSION, THE CSI PRESIDENT TAKES A DECISION THAT IS AS RADICAL AS IT IS UNEXPECTED.

GENTLEMEN, WE CANNOT CONTINUE USING AEROFOILS LIKE THIS. I'VE MADE THE DECISION TO BAN THEM WITH IMMEDIATE EFFECT! THE NEW RULE WILL TAKE EFFECT AT THE NEXT GRAND PRIX.

IMPOSSIBLE!

IT'S APPALLING...

IT'S IRRESPONSIBLE TO DECIDE THIS IN THE MIDDLE OF A GRAND PRIX WEEKEND...

NO CONSULTATION!

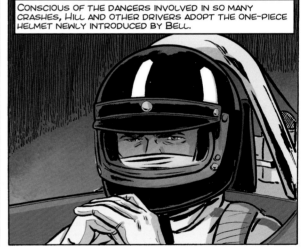

CONSCIOUS OF THE DANGERS INVOLVED IN SO MANY CRASHES, HILL AND OTHER DRIVERS ADOPT THE ONE-PIECE HELMET NEWLY INTRODUCED BY BELL.

AS USUAL, THERE'S A STREAM OF RETIREMENTS DURING THE RACE. GRAHAM, DRIVING HIS 1968 CAR, TAKES HIS RECORD OF MONACO WINS TO FIVE. SIFFERT FINISHES THIRD IN THE ROB WALKER TEAM'S LOTUS. RICHARD ATTWOOD, REPLACING RINDT AT THE LAST MINUTE, FINISHES IN A CREDITABLE FOURTH PLACE. THE TWO MATRAS HAVE TO RETIRE.

FANTASTIC, GRAHAM! THERE WERE THREE LOTUSES IN THE FIRST FOUR!

23

IN MAY, THE CHAPMAN FAMILY MOVES INTO EAST CARLETON MANOR, NEAR NORWICH AND NEAR LOTUS'S FACTORY AT HETHEL. THE PLANS WERE DRAWN BY COLIN HIMSELF AND THE HOUSE TOOK THREE YEARS TO BUILD.

WE'VE COME A LONG WAY TOGETHER, COLIN!

I'M SO HAPPY I COULD DO ALL THIS FOR YOU...

AND NOW, WITH THE LITTLE GRASS AIRSTRIP BEHIND THE HOUSE, I'LL BE ABLE TO USE MY PLANE TO GET BACK MORE QUICKLY AFTER EACH RACE.

THE DUTCH GP. IN THE PADDOCK, THE NEW LOTUS 63 CREATES A SENSATION. ITS FOUR-WHEEL-DRIVE LAYOUT DRAWS ON THE LOTUS 56 DESIGNED FOR INDIANAPOLIS.

Grand Prix
zaterdag 21 juni
zandvoort

LOTUS 63:
FORD COSWORTH DFV,
V8 ENGINE, 2,993CC
FOUR VALVES PER CYLINDER
FOUR OHC, DIRECT INJECTION
410BHP AT 9,000RPM
FIVE-SPEED GEARBOX
FOUR-WHEEL DRIVE
MONOCOQUE ALUMINIUM CHASSIS
600KG

I THINK FOUR-WHEEL DRIVE IS THE FUTURE IN F1.

YOU'RE NOT THE ONLY TEAM WORKING ON IT, THOUGH.

IT'S TOTALLY DIFFERENT TO DRIVE. AND IT VIBRATES CONSTANTLY.

AFTER A FEW LAPS AT MODERATE SPEED, HILL DECIDES TO GO BACK TO HIS GOOD OLD 49B.

COLIN, THE 63 IS NOWHERE NEAR READY YET...

I'M NOT DRIVING THAT DEATH TRAP EITHER!

24

IN THE END, RINDT AND HILL TAKE POLE AND THIRD FASTEST TIME.

RAAAA
AAAA

BUT DURING THE RACE, RINDT HAS TO RETIRE WITH TRANSMISSION PROBLEMS. GRAHAM FINISHES ONLY SEVENTH. STEWART WINS AGAIN.

I COULDN'T DO ANY BETTER. THE CAR JUST WASN'T RUNNING PROPERLY.

WITH RENÉ BOVY, REPRESENTING THE SPA CIRCUIT, JACKIE STEWART ASSESSES THE TRACK A FEW WEEKS BEFORE THE GP.

HERE, AT STAVELOT, WE MUST HAVE CRASH BARRIERS. WE COME DOWN HERE AT 175MPH. IT'S TOO DANGEROUS IF SOMEONE COMES OFF THE TRACK!

IMPOSSIBLE!

33 VP 3

IT WOULD BE TOO EXPENSIVE AND NOT READY IN TIME FOR THE GRAND PRIX!

FOR THE FIRST TIME AN F1 GRAND PRIX WOULD BE BOYCOTTED BY THE DRIVERS.

IN THAT CASE, I CAN TELL YOU RIGHT NOW THAT THE DRIVERS WON'T BE RACING HERE THIS YEAR. IT'S OUT OF THE QUESTION FOR US TO RISK 1966 ALL OVER AGAIN.

33 VP 3

AT SPA, THREE YEARS EARLIER.

WHILE THE TRACK WAS DRY AT THE START, THERE WAS A SUDDEN DOWNPOUR AROUND BURNENVILLE. WITHOUT WARNING, VISIBILITY WAS VIRTUALLY ZERO.

EIGHT DRIVERS CAME OFF THE TRACK AND THERE WERE NO BARRIERS TO STOP THEM ENDING UP ON A BANK, AMONG TREES OR EVEN NEAR HOUSES.

IT WAS RAINING SO HARD, I COULDN'T KEEP MY BRM ON THE TRACK...

25

The electric fuel pump carries on operating and petrol flows everywhere... One spark and everything will go up in flames.

Damn it, I can't get out!

Graham, quick! I'm trapped and petrol is leaking out. Get something to remove the steering wheel!

Twenty-five minutes later, Hill and Bob Bondurant manage to get Stewart out of the car. There's still no sign of the emergency teams.

Stewart has hurt his back and ribs. Hill and Bondurant remove his petrol-soaked clothes as they're burning his skin.

Graham, I think I may have arrived in heaven...

Quickly, turn away, sisters!

Goodness!

Dear Jesus!

26

The ambulance finally arrived 50 minutes after the crash. But the ambulance driver and the motorcycle escort leading us got lost on the way to the hospital. We didn't get there until two hours after my crash.

Stewart was brought back to England that evening in a private jet specially chartered by BRM's boss. His ongoing commitment to the GPDA is hardly surprising.

HILL AND RINDT ARE STILL REFUSING TO DRIVE THE LOTUS 63. CHAPMAN HAS TURNED TO JOHN MILES, A YOUNG DRIVER HE ADMIRES AND WHOM HE'S ENTERED SUCCESSFULLY IN DIFFERENT CATEGORIES.

THE RACE TURNS OUT TO BE A DISASTER: MILES RETIRES AFTER THE FIRST LAP, WITH A FAULTY FUEL PUMP.

AND RINDT, STILL SUFFERING AFTER HIS ACCIDENT AT BARCELONA, PULLS OUT HALFWAY THROUGH.

THE FRENCH GP TAKES PLACE AT THE CHARADE CIRCUIT, OUTSIDE CLERMONT-FERRAND. FIVE MILES LONG, IT'S A 'MINI NÜRBURGRING' WITH 51 BENDS AND STEEP GRADIENTS. THERE ARE JUST 13 CARS ENTERED.

STEWART TAKES HIS FOURTH WIN OF THE SEASON IN STYLE, AHEAD OF BELTOISE AND ICKX; HILL MANAGES ONLY SIXTH PLACE.

AT THE BRITISH GP AT SILVERSTONE, IT'S CLEAR THAT LOTUS HAS SOME IMITATORS. MCLAREN AND MATRA HAVE FOUR-WHEEL-DRIVE CARS: THE M9A DRIVEN BY DEREK BELL AND THE MS84 DRIVEN BY JEAN-PIERRE BELTOISE.

27

AS FOR TEAM LOTUS, A SURPRISE AWAITS GRAHAM AND JOCHEN, BUT IT'S NOT A WELCOME ONE.

GENTLEMEN, YOUR CARS!

THE 63s?

THAT'S RIGHT. I SOLD YOUR TWO 49Bs TO JO BONNIER AND JOHN LOVE!

HILL AND RINDT WON'T TAKE IT LYING DOWN. THEY INSIST ON CHAPMAN RUNNING BONNIER'S 49B AND THE SPARE CAR. RELATIONS BETWEEN THE TWO DRIVERS AND COLIN ARE AT A LOW.

JO, WE'VE BEEN FRIENDS FOR YEARS... PLEASE LEND ME THE 49B YOU'VE JUST BOUGHT FROM COLIN!

OK WITH ME, BUT YOU'LL HAVE TO CLEAR IT WITH COLIN.

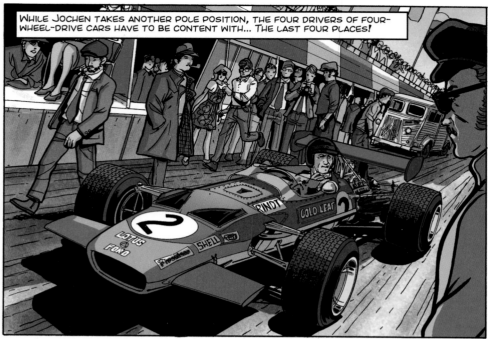

WHILE JOCHEN TAKES ANOTHER POLE POSITION, THE FOUR DRIVERS OF FOUR-WHEEL-DRIVE CARS HAVE TO BE CONTENT WITH... THE LAST FOUR PLACES!

IN THE RACE ITSELF, THE CROWD IS TREATED TO AN ENTHRALLING DUEL BETWEEN STEWART AND RINDT.

BUT JOCHEN HAS TO STOP TO CHANGE A REAR WHEEL, SO THE SCOT TAKES HIS FIFTH GP WIN OF THE YEAR. RINDT ONLY FINISHES FOURTH AND HILL IS SEVENTH.

EVEN WITH FIVE RACES STILL TO GO, I THINK THE CHAMPIONSHIP IS OUT OF OUR REACH...

YOU CAN SAY THAT AGAIN! THE 63 HAS RUINED THE SEASON FOR US...

MILES IN HIS 63 COMES HOME LAST, BEHIND BELTOISE'S FOUR-WHEEL-DRIVE MATRA. BONNIER'S 63 HAD TO RETIRE.

IT REALLY IS THE MOST DIFFICULT CAR I'VE HAD TO DRIVE.

IT'S LIKE A PNEUMATIC DRILL!

BUT FOUR-WHEEL-DRIVE HAS SUCH A LOT OF POTENTIAL. THIS ISN'T THE TIME TO GIVE UP ON ITS DEVELOPMENT!

RIGHT, IF THOSE TWO WON'T DRIVE THE 63, I'M GOING TO APPROACH OUR OLD FRIEND MARIO...

GOOD IDEA. THAT WAY, YOU'LL KNOW WHETHER YOU'RE RIGHT TO PERSEVERE WITH IT...

21 JULY 1969. COLIN HAS JOINED HIS FAMILY FOR A FEW DAYS AT THEIR IBIZA HOUSE.

IN THE SEARCH FOR NEW IDEAS, HE PORES OVER MAGAZINES AND BOOKS.

WHOOSSHHHHHHH...

ALWAYS THINKING ABOUT TECHNICAL ADVANCEMENTS, HE SHOWS THE CHILDREN HOW ROCKETS TAKE OFF FROM CAPE KENNEDY...

FOLLOWED BY ENTRY INTO LUNAR ORBIT.

NEXT, COLIN DEMONSTRATES HOW THE ASTRONAUTS LIE IN THE COMMAND MODULE AND EXPLAINS THEIR RESPECTIVE ROLES.

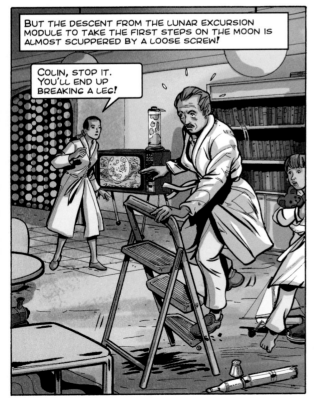

BUT THE DESCENT FROM THE LUNAR EXCURSION MODULE TO TAKE THE FIRST STEPS ON THE MOON IS ALMOST SCUPPERED BY A LOOSE SCREW!

COLIN, STOP IT. YOU'LL END UP BREAKING A LEG!

COLIN FINDS IT HARD TO COPE WITHOUT ORDER AND DISCIPLINE. FORTUNATELY, HE HAS HIS ATTACHÉ CASE CONTAINING A POCKET TORCH, PROPELLING PENCIL, FIRST-AID KIT, MINI CAMERA, SCREWDRIVER AND MANY OTHER ITEMS, EACH ONE WITH A DUPLICATE AND ALL NEATLY LAID OUT!

IT'S 3 O'CLOCK IN THE MORNING... A GOOD TIME TO WITNESS THIS HISTORIC MOMENT!

29

THE GERMAN GP AT THE NÜRBURGRING. ENGINE PROBLEMS DISRUPT ANDRETTI'S PRACTICE AND HE'S ONLY 14TH ON THE GRID. RINDT IN THE 49C IS AGAIN ON THE FRONT ROW NEXT TO ICKX AND STEWART.

THE MEAGRE LINE-UP OF F1 CARS IS FILLED OUT BY F2 CARS. DURING PRACTICE, GERHARD MITTER'S BMW 269 LOSES A WHEEL AND COMES OFF THE TRACK ON ONE OF THE MANY SPOTS WHERE THERE'S NO BARRIER. THE GERMAN DRIVER IS KILLED.

THE RACE TURNS OUT TO BE A COMPLETE FAILURE FOR LOTUS: ANDRETTI LOSES CONTROL OF HIS CAR AFTER GROUNDING IT ON THE FIRST LAP.

RINDT IS FORCED TO RETIRE MID-RACE WITH IGNITION PROBLEMS. HILL HAS TO SETTLE FOR FOURTH PLACE.

ICKX WINS BRILLIANTLY AHEAD OF STEWART.

AT THE ITALIAN GP, THE CROWD WITNESSES AN INCREDIBLE RACE WITH ITS OUTCOME IN DOUBT UNTIL THE LAST FEW METRES.

THE FIRST FOUR TO CROSS THE LINE ARE WITHIN 1/19TH OF A SECOND OF EACH OTHER. STEWART IS AHEAD OF RINDT, BELTOISE AND McLAREN.

30

STEWART TAKES THE DRIVERS' WORLD CHAMPIONSHIP FOR THE FIRST TIME, HAVING DOMINATED ALL SEASON.

WHAT A RACE! THERE WAS NOTHING BETWEEN THE FOUR OF US...

WELL DONE, JACKIE, FOR YOUR WIN AND THE TITLE!

AS FOR RINDT, HE IS HAPPY TO BE ON THE PODIUM AT LAST, FOR THE FIRST TIME DURING THE 1969 SEASON.

I HOPE YOU'LL SOON BE WINNING AGAIN...

AT THE CANADIAN GP, RINDT IS AGAIN ON THE PODIUM BEHIND ICKX AND BRABHAM. MATRA WINS THE CONSTRUCTORS' TITLE.

IT'S BEEN GOING BETTER LATELY!

FOR YOU, YES...

BUT NOT FOR GRAHAM...

HILL FINDS IT HARD TO TAKE BEING OUTSHONE BY HIS YOUNGER TEAM-MATE. HE'S SLOWER IN PRACTICE AND HIS RESULTS HAVE BEEN MEDIOCRE IN RECENT RACES.

US GRAND PRIX. RINDT TAKES POLE POSITION FOR THE FIFTH TIME THIS SEASON. HILL IS FOURTH, 0.4SEC BEHIND. ANDRETTI IS ONLY 13TH IN THE 63.

RINDT AND STEWART HAVE ANOTHER LENGTHY DUEL, WHICH ENDS AT ONE-THIRD DISTANCE WHEN THE SCOT HAS TO RETIRE WITH AN OIL LEAK.

HILL, WHO IS PLAGUED WITH ROADHOLDING PROBLEMS, SLIPS DOWN THE FIELD AND THEN SPINS OFF.

BUT HILL, HELPED BY THE DOWNWARD SLOPE TOWARDS THE TRACK, GETS HIS CAR GOING AGAIN.

A FEW LAPS BEFORE THE FINISH, HILL'S LOTUS LEAVES THE TRACK AT SPEED AFTER A TYRE BLOW-OUT.

HIS SEAT BELT HAS NOT BEEN RE-BUCKLED AFTER HIS SPIN.

RINDT FINALLY WINS AND IS BACK IN CONTENTION FOR THIRD PLACE IN THE WORLD CHAMPIONSHIP.

GRAHAM HILL HAS MULTIPLE LEG FRACTURES AND A DAMAGED NERVE. WILL HE BE ABLE TO RETURN TO RACING?

IN THE DOCTORS' OPINION, FULL RECOVERY TAKE TWO YEARS.

THE SEASON COMES TO AN ABRUPT END FOR TEAM LOTUS IN MEXICO. MILES'S 63 IS AGAIN LET DOWN BY ITS FUEL PUMP.

AND RINDT EXPERIENCES SUSPENSION PROBLEMS, RETIRING A THIRD OF THE WAY THROUGH THE RACE, WHICH IS WON BY HULME FROM ICKX.

MY GOD, WHAT A SEASON!

DESPITE A PROMISING END TO THE SEASON, RELATIONS BETWEEN CHAPMAN AND RINDT AREN'T LOOKING GOOD.

IT'S LUCKY YOU CAN COUNT ON RINDT.

I'M NOT SO SURE. BRABHAM IS TRYING TO GET HIM BACK. HE'S RAISING THE STAKES.

AND JOCHEN BLAMES ME FOR HAVING RUINED HIS SEASON BY SPENDING TOO MUCH TIME ON THE 63...

OH DEAR! IT'S NEVER SIMPLE.

I'VE DECIDED TO STOP PUTTING MONEY INTO THE 63, JABBY.

WE NEED TO ASSESS WHAT WENT WRONG.

THE 63'S DESIGN IS THE RESULT OF COLLABORATION BETWEEN LOTUS AND FERGUSON. BECAUSE OF THE TIGHT FIT, THE ENGINE IS TURNED THROUGH 180° AND THE GEARBOX IS LOCATED UNDER THE DRIVER'S SEAT, WITH THE MIDDLE DIFFERENTIAL ON THE LEFT AND THE TWO TRANSMISSION SHAFTS LINKING THE FRONT AND REAR DIFFERENTIALS.

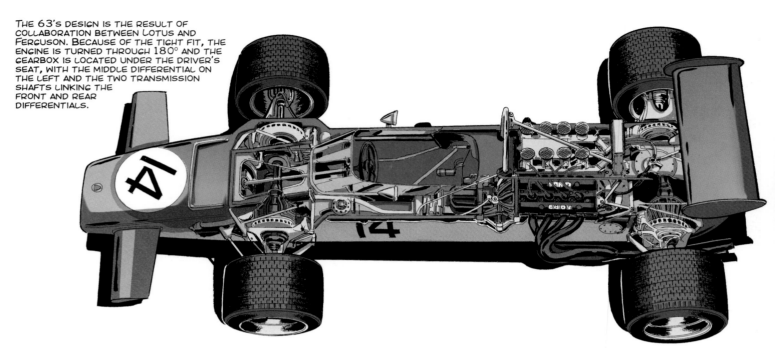

FOUR-WHEEL-DRIVE TECHNOLOGY IS PERFECT FOR INDIANAPOLIS OR WHEN GRIP IS POOR. DO YOU REMEMBER THE PERFORMANCE OF THE FERGUSON P99 F1 CAR IN THE WET?

IN 1961, STIRLING MOSS HAD A BRILLIANT WIN DRIVING THE FERGUSON P99, THE FIRST FOUR-WHEEL-DRIVE F1 CAR, IN THE INTERNATIONAL GOLD CUP, A NON-CHAMPIONSHIP RACE THAT TOOK PLACE IN THE RAIN AT OULTON PARK.

HAD IT RAINED AS MUCH THIS YEAR AS LAST, THE 63 WOULD HAVE WON QUITE A FEW GRANDS PRIX!

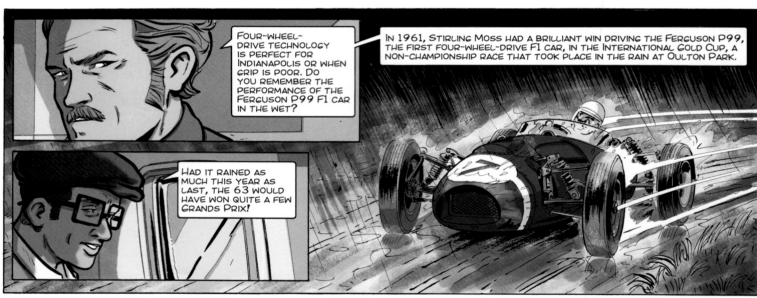

ON A DRY SURFACE, THE DRIVER STRUGGLES TO FIND THE RIGHT BALANCE WHEN ACCELERATING HARD OUT OF A BEND.*

YES, MILES TOLD ME HE HAD TO ADJUST HIS DRIVING STYLE...

EXACTLY. IT'S IMPOSSIBLE TO MAKE FULL USE OF THE ENGINE POWER AND CONTROL ANY OVERSTEER USING THE ACCELERATOR AND STEERING WHEEL.

MATRA AND MCLAREN HAVE BEEN STRUGGLING WITH THE SAME PROBLEMS... NOT THAT IT'S MUCH CONSOLATION!

THE 63 HAS ANOTHER DRAWBACK – ITS WEIGHT. IT WEIGHS 100KG MORE THAN THE LOTUS 49.

GRAHAM AND JOCHEN HAVEN'T HELPED. BUT I HAVE TO ACCEPT THAT THE CAR IS NOT POWERFUL ENOUGH ON A DRY SURFACE...

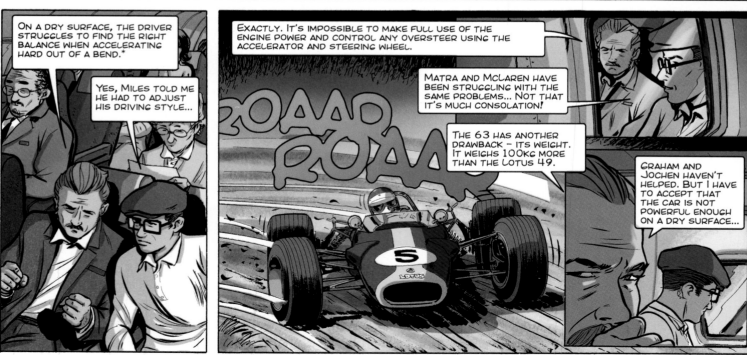

* IN 1969, FOUR-WHEEL-DRIVE SYSTEMS WERE NOT AS SOPHISTICATED AS NOWADAYS, ESPECIALLY IN LACKING TODAY'S ELECTRONICS.

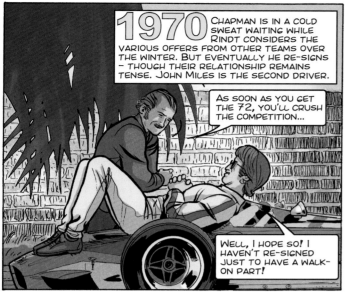

1970 CHAPMAN IS IN A COLD SWEAT WAITING WHILE RINDT CONSIDERS THE VARIOUS OFFERS FROM OTHER TEAMS OVER THE WINTER. BUT EVENTUALLY HE RE-SIGNS – THOUGH THEIR RELATIONSHIP REMAINS TENSE. JOHN MILES IS THE SECOND DRIVER.

AS SOON AS YOU GET THE 72, YOU'LL CRUSH THE COMPETITION...

WELL, I HOPE SO! I HAVEN'T RE-SIGNED JUST TO HAVE A WALK-ON PART!

GRAHAM HILL SURPRISES EVERYONE WITH HIS SWIFT RETURN, AFTER SPENDING THE WINTER IN PHYSIOTHERAPY. HE HAS RELUCTANTLY LEFT TEAM LOTUS FOR ROB WALKER'S TEAM, WHERE HE'LL DRIVE A LOTUS 49C.

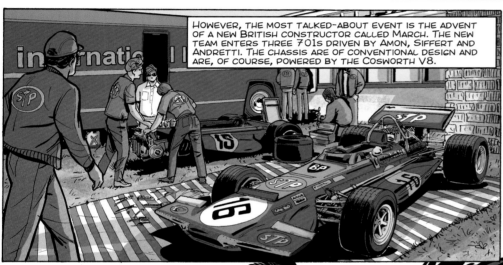

HOWEVER, THE MOST TALKED-ABOUT EVENT IS THE ADVENT OF A NEW BRITISH CONSTRUCTOR CALLED MARCH. THE NEW TEAM ENTERS THREE 701s DRIVEN BY AMON, SIFFERT AND ANDRETTI. THE CHASSIS ARE OF CONVENTIONAL DESIGN AND ARE, OF COURSE, POWERED BY THE COSWORTH V8.

MATRA DECIDES TO GO ITS OWN WAY, WITH BELTOISE AND PESCAROLO, USING THE V12 ENGINE. 'UNCLE KEN' HAS TO MAKE THE BEST OF A BAD JOB: HE WOULD RUN STEWART AND SERVOZ-GAVIN IN COSWORTH-POWERED MARCH 701s IN HIS OWN COLOURS.

WHAT DO YOU THINK OF IT COMPARED WITH THE MS80?

THE CHASSIS IS GOOD, THE V12 TERRIFIC. SHEER MUSIC!

IN PRACTICE FOR THE SOUTH AFRICAN GP, MARCH SURPRISES EVERYONE BY TAKING THE FIRST TWO PLACES ON THE GRID THANKS TO STEWART AND AMON. WITH A NUMBER OF LOCAL DRIVERS, THE FIELD NUMBERS 23 ENTRIES – THE BEST FOR A LONG TIME.

VROOOAAARROOAAAA
ROOAAAA VROOAAAA
ROOAAAA ROOAAAA

THE SCOT LEADS AT THE START, BUT IS QUICKLY JOINED BY BRABHAM AND HULME.

32

JACK BRABHAM EVENTUALLY WINS, AHEAD OF HULME AND STEWART.

RINDT HAD A SCRAPE WITH ANOTHER CAR AND THEN HIS ENGINE SEIZED. MILES GAINS HIS FIRST POINTS, FINISHING FIFTH AHEAD OF THE HEROIC HILL.

SPANISH GP. THE NEW LOTUS-
COSWORTH 72 IS ATTRACTING
ALL THE ATTENTION. ITS DESIGN IS
THE WORK OF COLIN CHAPMAN AND
MAURICE PHILIPPE. TO HELP SHIFT
THE CENTRE OF GRAVITY
REARWARDS, THE 72 HAS
TWO SMALL RADIATORS
FITTED TO ITS FLANKS.

THE 72'S DESIGN IS ALSO WELL
AHEAD OF THE COMPETITION
AERODYNAMICALLY; THE THREE-
DECK, WEDGE-SHAPED REAR
AEROFOIL, INSPIRED BY
THAT OF THE 63, IS A GOOD
EXAMPLE.

THE FRONT AND REAR BRAKES ARE INBOARD, AND
THE RISING-RATE TORSION-BAR SUSPENSION HAS AN
ANTI-DIVE SET-UP AT THE FRONT AND ANTI-SQUAT
AT THE REAR. CHAPMAN HAS PERSUADED FIRESTONE
TO PROVIDE SPECIAL TYRES FOR THE CAR.

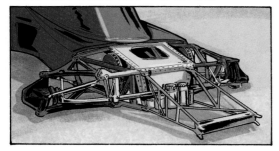

LOTUS 72:
FORD-COSWORTH DFV ENGINE
90° V8, 2,993cc
FOUR VALVES PER CYLINDER
FOUR OHC, DIRECT INJECTION
430BHP AT 10,000RPM
FIVE-SPEED GEARBOX
ALUMINIUM MONOCOQUE CHASSIS
540KG

SINCE THE START OF THE F1 WORLD CHAMPIONSHIP IN 1950,
EACH GP ORGANISER HAD DECIDED WHO IT WOULD INVITE TO
ITS RACE AND HOW STARTING MONEY WOULD BE AWARDED,
ACCORDING TO THE RECORD OF THE TEAMS AND DRIVERS.

LIKE ALL THE OTHER TEAMS IN
THE FORMULA 1 CONSTRUCTORS'
ASSOCIATION, YOU WILL HAVE ONE
DRIVER WITH AN AUTOMATIC ENTRY.

THAT WILL BE
JOCHEN RINDT.

STARTING WITH
THE 1970 SPANISH
GP, THE 'GENEVA
AGREEMENT' BRINGS
MAJOR CHANGES. SOME
TEAMS AND DRIVERS
HAVE DEFINITE ENTRIES
FOR THE WHOLE
SEASON; OTHERS NOW
HAVE TO QUALIFY.
THE STARTING-MONEY
SCALES ARE ALSO
COMPLETELY REVISED.

WHAT ABOUT
PRIZE MONEY?

PRIZE MONEY WILL NOW BE RELATED
TO RACE POSITION AT ONE-THIRD
DISTANCE, TWO-THIRDS DISTANCE
AND THE FINISH.

YOUR SECOND
DRIVER SHOULD
QUALIFY.

HOW MANY
DRIVERS WILL
THERE BE IN
THE RACE?

ER...
LET ME
SEE...

BUT IN SPAIN, THE NUMBER OF COMPETITORS IS LIMITED TO 17, BECAUSE OF THE SHORT
CIRCUIT. WITH THE NEW RULES NOT HAVING BEEN PROPERLY TRIALLED, IT'S UNCLEAR WHICH
DRIVERS WILL BE TAKING PART UNTIL A FEW MINUTES BEFORE THE START.

36

On the second lap, Ickx's Ferrari is hit by Oliver's BRM. With a full fuel tank, the Ferrari instantly bursts into flames.

Rindt retires on the tenth lap with ignition problems. Only five cars finish. Stewart wins the race in his March.

How is Ickx?

He's OK. Incredibly, he escaped with just a few burns...

The Monaco GP. Rindt has been unhappy with the 72's anti-dive and anti-squat systems, so Chapman decides to use the old 49C as a stop-gap for this race. Rindt starts eighth and Miles fails to qualify.

MONACO / 10 MAI 1970

programme officiel

Led alternately by Stewart and Brabham, the Grand Prix reaches an exciting climax.

Rindt, the bit between his teeth, makes huge inroads into Brabham's lead in the final laps.

'Black Jack', thinking Rindt is just behind him, leaves his braking late for the last corner of the last lap!

37

RINDT TAKES HIS 49C TO A MAGNIFICENT VICTORY, AHEAD OF BRABHAM AND PESCAROLO.

THERE'S FURTHER TRAGEDY ON 6 JUNE: BRUCE MCLAREN, THIRD IN THE 1969 WORLD CHAMPIONSHIP, IS KILLED AT GOODWOOD TESTING THE MCLAREN M8C CAN-AM CAR. HIS TEAM WILL SURVIVE HIM...

THE LOTUS 72C APPEARS AT THE DUTCH GRAND PRIX, WITH CONVENTIONAL SUSPENSION. THE ANTI-DIVE FEATURE TENDED TO CAUSE LOCKING OF THE FRONT BRAKES AND THE ANTI-SQUAT SYSTEM REDUCED TRACTION.

WHY HAVE YOU DECIDED TO DROP THE FRONT ANTI-DIVE SYSTEM?

JOCHEN THINKS THERE'S BETTER HANDLING 'FEEL' WITH CONVENTIONAL SUSPENSION.

RINDT TAKES POLE POSITION. THE NEXT DAY, HE WINS THE RACE, CRUSHING THE COMPETITION. STEWART AND ICKX ARE ALSO ON THE PODIUM. BUT FOR TWO-THIRDS OF THE RACE, A BURNING CAR CASTS A PALL OVER THE TRACK.

ON THE 23RD LAP, THE WILLIAMS TEAM'S DE TOMASO CAR, DRIVEN BY PIERS COURAGE, SOMERSAULTED OFF THE TRACK. THE DRIVER WAS TRAPPED UNDER THE OVERTURNED CAR, WHICH INSTANTLY BURST INTO FLAMES – AND COURAGE IS DEAD.

AS RINDT MOUNTS THE PODIUM, HE DOESN'T FEEL LIKE CELEBRATING. COLIN HAS GIVEN HIM THE SAD NEWS.

I'VE HAD ENOUGH OF SEEING ALL OUR FRIENDS DISAPPEAR!

SO HAVE I... NINA, IF I WIN THE TITLE, I PROMISE I'LL HANG UP MY HELMET AT THE END OF THE SEASON.

38

CHAMPIONNAT DU MONDE
DES CONDUCTEURS F1
GRAND PRIX DE FRANCE
CLERMONT-FD
BP

5 JUILLET
1970

PROGRAMME OFFICIEL 3F

RINDT WINS THE NEXT THREE GRANDS PRIX, AT CLERMONT-FERRAND, BRANDS HATCH AND HOCKENHEIM. CHAPMAN IS ONCE AGAIN OVERJOYED THAT ANOTHER OF HIS DESIGNS HAS TRIUMPHED.

BRITISH GRAND PRIX
Brands Hatch
18 July 1970
Official Programme

Sponsored by
DAILY MAIL

2. August 13.⁰⁰Uhr AvD

Grosser Preis
von
WELTMEISTERSCHAFT
Deutschland
MOTODROM HOCKENHEIM

JOHN MILES SENSES THAT HIS DAYS WITH TEAM LOTUS ARE NUMBERED DESPITE HIS INVALUABLE CONTRIBUTION TO THE 72'S DEVELOPMENT.

CLEARLY, JOCHEN WITH HIS FIVE WINS ALREADY LOOKS UNASSAILABLE IN THE WORLD CHAMPIONSHIP. WAY BEHIND HIM, BRABHAM, HULME, STEWART, ICKX AND RODRIGUEZ APPEAR DESTINED TO REMAIN ALSO-RANS. MATHEMATICALLY, HOWEVER, NOTHING IS YET DECIDED.

39

FOR THE AUSTRIAN GP, RINDT TAKES POLE. THE CROWD, WHO HAVE TURNED UP IN FORCE AT THE NEW ZELTWEG CIRCUIT, EXPECT TO SEE THEIR IDOL TAKE THE RACE AND THE WORLD CHAMPIONSHIP.

JOCHEN, DO WE NEED ANY FINAL TWEAKS?

NO, THE CAR'S ABSOLUTELY PERFECT. EVEN A MONKEY COULD WIN WITH IT!

BUT RINDT RETIRES WITH ENGINE TROUBLE AND THE SCARLET FERRARIS OF ICKX AND REGAZZONI ARE VICTORIOUS.

I DO FEEL FOR JOCHEN...

I'M SURE HE'LL TAKE THE TITLE AT MONZA!

ITALIAN GP, FRIDAY 4 SEPTEMBER. THE MECHANICS ARE EXHAUSTED BY RELENTLESS WORK IN RECENT WEEKS.

MO DI MONZA

41° gran premio d'Italia

TWO NEW 72Cs HAVE BEEN HURRIEDLY BUILT, ONE FOR THE 23-YEAR-OLD EMERSON FITTIPALDI, WHO, AFTER MANY ACHIEVEMENTS IN F3, HAS SIGNED AS LOTUS'S THIRD DRIVER. THE OTHER IS FOR GRAHAM HILL, NOW ROB WALKER'S DRIVER.

THE FIRST QUALIFYING SESSION. AT MONZA, IT'S THE CAR'S TOP SPEED THAT COUNTS, BECAUSE LONG STRAIGHTS PREDOMINATE AT THE ITALIAN TRACK.

1M 25.71S. IT'S TOO SLOW! YOU'RE 1.1SEC BEHIND ICKX.

I DON'T HAVE THE TOP SPEED.

AS AN AERODYNAMIC SOLUTION, THEY CAN EITHER USE FLAT AEROFOILS OR REMOVE THEM ALTOGETHER.

REMOVE THE AEROFOILS.

WITH THIS NEW SET-UP, RINDT INCREASES HIS TOP SPEED AND GAINS A FEW EXTRA TENTHS OF A SECOND. BUT THE LOTUS, WITHOUT DOWNFORCE, IS NOW VERY UNSTABLE.

COLIN ASKS DAVE 'BEAKY' SIMS, HIS MECHANIC, TO MAKE THE SAME CHANGE TO MILES'S CAR.

GET RID OF HIS AEROFOILS. IT'S THE ONLY WAY TO GET A DECENT TIME...

NO, COLIN!

IT'S THE ONLY WAY TO GET IT TO GO FAST ENOUGH!

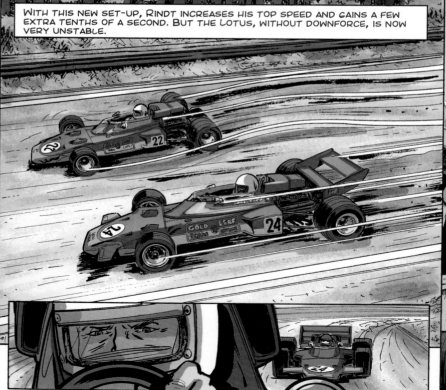

40

THE CAR IS JUST UNDRIVEABLE!

JOHN, LESS THAN THREE YEARS AGO, NO F1 CARS HAD AEROFOILS... YOU'LL RACE WITHOUT THEM.

OUT OF THE QUESTION.

THAT'S AN ORDER!

On Friday evening, Jochen is dining in style and good company at a famous hotel in Monza.

HOW MANY MORE REVS DID YOU GAIN WITHOUT AEROFOILS THIS AFTERNOON?

600RPM. THAT'S NO SECRET. WE HAVE TO DRIVE WITHOUT THEM...

I SAW YOU AT ASCARI... THE CAR WAS ALL OVER THE PLACE.

IT'S THE ONLY WAY TO BEAT THE FERRARIS AND TAKE THIS WORLD CHAMPIONSHIP TITLE...

I'VE ASKED COLIN TO PUT IN A LONGER FIFTH GEAR FOR TOMORROW!

AND HE'S ALSO GIVEN YOU A FRESH ENGINE...

I REALLY WANT TO STOP RACING. I WANT TO MOVE ON TO OTHER THINGS...

SURE! BUT WHAT DO YOU THINK YOU'D DO IF YOU RETIRE?

I WILL HAVE A RANGE OF SPORTS CLOTHING UNDER MY NAME.

IT'S AN INTERESTING PROJECT AND I THINK IT'LL WORK WELL.

I'M GOING TO WIN THIS GP, TAKE THE TITLE... AND THEN A CHANGE OF LIFESTYLE...

41

SATURDAY 5 SEPTEMBER, SECOND PRACTICE SESSION. THE NEW GEAR RATIO INCREASES TOP SPEED BY 15MPH.

THERE'S NOTHING LEFT OF THE FRONT OF JOCHEN'S CAR.

HULME STOPS AT THE PITS TO TELL CHAPMAN.

JOCHEN WAS TAKEN BY HELICOPTER STRAIGHT TO THE NIGUARDA HOSPITAL, NORTH OF MILAN.

'EMERGENCY', IT'S THIS WAY.

BRM'S LOUIS STANLEY IS THERE. HE TAKES NINA ASIDE TO BREAK THE TERRIBLE NEWS.

FOLLOWING RINDT'S DEATH, TEAM LOTUS AND ROB WALKER'S TEAM PULL OUT.

JOCHEN'S CAR IS SEIZED FOR THE ENQUIRY. IN ACCORDANCE WITH THE ITALIAN PENAL CODE, CHAPMAN IS CHARGED WITH HOMICIDE.

HE GOES HOME AND JUST SITS, DEVASTATED, FOR DAYS.

43

Team Lotus stays away from the Canadian GP as a mark of respect. Ickx wins the race.

JACKY, YOU'VE GOT TWO GRANDS PRIX LEFT. IF YOU WIN BOTH, YOU CAN STILL WIN THE TITLE.

IT WON'T BE EASY. LOTUS WILL BE BACK FOR THE NEXT GRAND PRIX.

For the US GP, Miles, shocked by Rindt's death, is left out. Fittipaldi makes up the team with the Swedish driver Reine Wisell making his F1 debut. In practice Fittipaldi impresses with his third place behind Ickx and Stewart. Wisell doesn't do badly either, with ninth on the grid.

EMERSON REALLY IMPRESSED ME!

WELL, LET'S SEE...

During the race, Stewart leads from Ickx, who has to stop with fuel problems. Then Stewart retires after his Tyrrell 001 develops engine trouble. Rodriguez then takes the lead ahead of Fittipaldi.

Ickx, resuming 12th, gradually makes up ground. Seven laps from the finish, Rodriguez has to stop for fuel.

Eventually, Fittipaldi wins the GP ahead of Rodriguez, Wisell and Ickx. Thanks to the Brazilian's victory, Rindt is named World Champion, though sadly, and uniquely, it is a posthumous title.

THANK YOU ON BEHALF OF JOCHEN!

DON'T YOU REGRET HAVING MISSED THE TITLE BY SO LITTLE?

I DON'T THINK I WOULD HAVE ENJOYED BEATING A DRIVER WE'VE LOST SO TRAGICALLY... I WAS LUCKY MYSELF TO GET OUT ALIVE IN SPAIN!

JOHN MILES HAS ENDURED A DIFFICULT SEASON WITH ITS CONSTANT STRAINS. DISMISSED BY LOTUS, HE BECOMES A TEST DRIVER AT BRM, BEFORE TURNING TO OTHER RACING CATEGORIES.

GRAHAM HILL, STILL AFFECTED BY HIS SERIOUS CRASH IN LATE 1969, FINISHES ONLY 13TH IN THE CHAMPIONSHIP WITH JUST SEVEN POINTS. HE GETS READY TO LEAVE THE ROB WALKER TEAM FOR BRABHAM.

CONGRATULATIONS ON ANOTHER TITLE, COLIN!

THANKS GRAHAM. BUT IT'S BEEN A SEASON I'D RATHER FORGET...

SADLY, DESPITE THE PROGRESS MADE TO IMPROVE SAFETY, THE 1970 SEASON HAS ONCE AGAIN TAKEN A TERRIBLE TOLL. THERE IS A LOT OF WORK STILL TO BE DONE BY THE GPDA AND THE FIA.

WE'LL HAVE TO BE MUCH FIRMER WITH THE ORGANISERS.

AND WITH THE CONSTRUCTORS AS WELL. THE CARS MUST BE MADE STRONGER.

AS FOR THE LOTUS GROUP, THE 72'S WINS AND THE NEW CONSTRUCTORS' WORLD CHAMPIONSHIP TITLE HAVE BOOSTED SALES AND PROFITS, MUCH TO THE DELIGHT OF EVERYONE THERE, FROM EMPLOYEES TO SHAREHOLDERS.

CHAPMAN IS CLEARLY AS GOOD AT BUSINESS AS HE IS AT DESIGNING INNOVATIVE RACING CARS.

CHAPMAN PREPARES TO RENEW THE FITTIPALDI/WISELL PARTNERSHIP FOR THE COMING 1971 SEASON, USING THE 72 THAT HAS SHOWN SO MUCH POTENTIAL. YET, ONCE AGAIN AFFECTED BY THE DEATH OF ONE OF HIS DRIVERS, HIS RELATIONSHIP WITH THEM REMAINS DISTANT.

MUCH ABSORBED BY HIS WORK, COLIN RARELY HAS ENOUGH TIME TO SPEND WITH HIS FAMILY.

In Italy the enquiry into Rindt's crash ended a year and a half later. It showed that the crash had been caused by the failure of the front right brake shaft. Still-cold tyres hadn't helped Rindt to control his car as it suddenly veered off the track to the left.

The front left wheel had gone under the barrier, from which bolts were missing. The front of the Lotus had been smashed by a concrete loudspeaker post.

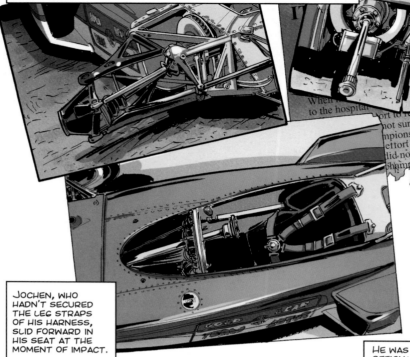

Jochen, who hadn't secured the leg straps of his harness, slid forward in his seat at the moment of impact.

MONZA 1970.

He was almost certainly killed on the spot, although it had been officially announced that he had died on the way to hospital.

December 1970.

Nina, I will remember Jochen as a fine man. And he will always be thought of as a great champion.

On behalf of the FIA, I present you with the Drivers' World Championship trophy, sadly awarded posthumously to Mr Jochen Rindt.

Colin receives the Constructors' trophy for the fourth time since 1963. He has achieved his ambition to dominate F1.

But this title has a bitter taste... He must move on.

Colin is just 42 years old. His rise has been meteoric. He is always ready to do battle and knows he must keep innovating if he is to achieve further victories and more World Championship titles.

Let me tell you about my latest idea!

I'm ready for anything...

46

1971

The Lotus 72 is the best car in Formula 1. Yet Colin Chapman, as committed to innovation as ever, has spent months devoting all his energy to the 56B, an F1 version of the gas-turbine 56 that raced at Indianapolis.

Lotus 56B:
Pratt & Whitney STN 6/76
Turbine
500bhp
Single-speed transmission
Four-wheel drive
Aluminium monocoque chassis
Firestone tyres
600kg

Early testing is inconclusive: Dave Walker retires after coming off the track in the Dutch GP and Reine Wisell finishes 11 laps behind the winner in the British GP.

Aware of the risks they could be running because of the inquiry into Rindt's death the year before, Chapman and Team Lotus stay away from Monza.

Chris Amon has set the best time in his Matra V12.

It isn't responsive enough!

Only one Lotus 56B is entered, driven by Emerson Fittipaldi for the mysterious 'World Wide Racing' managed by Peter Warr.

Keep your foot on the accelerator while braking...

You were 18th, 22.78 seconds behind pole...

It's a very heavy car...

Fittipaldi finishes in eighth place – a very respectable result.

The turbine wasn't working well because of the heat...

We'll talk to Colin about it.

AFTER DEBRIEFING AT THE FACTORY, CHAPMAN DECIDES, AGAINST ALL EXPECTATIONS, TO HALT DEVELOPMENT OF THE 56B.

IF WE DO WIN ANY RACES, I SUSPECT THE FIA WILL BAN TURBINES...

AT WATKINS GLEN, IT'S TIME TO TAKE STOCK. WITHOUT A WIN FOR THE FIRST SEASON SINCE 1959, LOTUS IS ONLY FIFTH IN THE CONSTRUCTORS' CHAMPIONSHIP.

FITTIPALDI, SIXTH IN A CHAMPIONSHIP DOMINATED BY STEWART AND TYRRELL, WANTS TO KNOW WHAT'S HAPPENING.

WHICH CAR WILL WE BE RACING NEXT SEASON?

WHAT! THE 72 AGAIN?

THE 72.

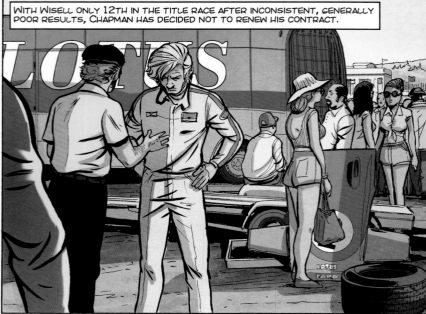

WITH WISELL ONLY 12TH IN THE TITLE RACE AFTER INCONSISTENT, GENERALLY POOR RESULTS, CHAPMAN HAS DECIDED NOT TO RENEW HIS CONTRACT.

AT THE SAME TIME, THE MANUFACTURE OF RACING CARS FOR PRIVATE TEAMS CEASES AT THE END OF 1971. THE 69 IS THE LAST OF THE LINE.

WHY ARE YOU STOPPING?

IT'S NO LONGER PROFITABLE FOR US TO BUILD CARS FOR FORMULA FORD, F3 AND F2...

1972

Among other developments, Team Lotus's sponsor has decided to promote a different brand...

I THINK THOSE COLOURS LOOK SUPERB!

I COULDN'T AGREE MORE...

John Player Team Lotus

And Dave Walker, who has won many F3 races with Lotus, replaces Wisell as the second driver.

WELL, DAVE, HERE YOU ARE IN THE BIG POOL! IT'S OVER TO YOU!

The tyre wars between Firestone and Goodyear continue...

SO YOU'VE FINALLY DECIDED TO STICK WITH FIRESTONE?

YES, THEY'VE DEVELOPED NEW TYRES ESPECIALLY FOR THE 72.

Emerson Fittipaldi wins five of the 12 Grands Prix: Spanish, Belgian, British, Austrian and Italian.

YOU SEE, COLIN, IT REALLY PAYS TO CONCENTRATE ON DEVELOPMENT...

YES, BUT I FIND IT LESS REWARDING THAN CREATING SOMETHING FROM SCRATCH!

At 25, Fittipaldi is the youngest Drivers' Champion. Stewart finishes second.

WELL DONE, EMERSON! DO YOU KNOW WHOSE RECORD YOU BROKE?

NO!

JIM CLARK!

sport-auto

Chapman au sommet de son art !

COLIN CHAPMA

Emerson vence e é campeâo

AND TEAM LOTUS TAKE ITS FIFTH CONSTRUCTORS' TITLE.

3

SALES OF PRODUCTION LOTUS CARS RIDE THE WAVE CREATED BY THE RACING TRIUMPHS, TO THE DELIGHT OF SALES MANAGER GRAHAM ARNOLD.

GRAHAM, CONGRATULATIONS ON THE SALES FIGURES!

YES, IT'S VERY GRATIFYING. I THINK THE F1 SUCCESS REALLY MAKES A DIFFERENCE!

'LOTUS ENGINEERING' HAS BEEN ESTABLISHED TO OFFER MANUFACTURERS ACCESS TO LOTUS'S KNOW-HOW IN CHASSIS AND ENGINE DESIGN.

OUR ENGINEERS ARE UP TO THEIR EYES IN WORK!

THE BRAND-NEW JENSEN-HEALEY USES THE 2-LITRE TYPE 907 ENGINE DEVELOPED BY THE NEW DEPARTMENT.

WE CERTAINLY HAVE A LOT OF GOOD NEWS AT THE MOMENT...

JENSEN IS ORDERING MORE ENGINES THAN EXPECTED... THE CAR IS SELLING REALLY WELL.

COLIN DIVERSIFIES HIS ACTIVITIES BY PERSONALLY BUYING THE MOONRAKER AND JCL MARINE BOATYARDS.

THIS IS THE MOONRAKER YARD I TOLD YOU ABOUT, HAZEL...

DON'T YOU HAVE ENOUGH TO DO ALREADY?

COLIN DEVELOPS A REVOLUTIONARY VACUUM-MOULDING PROCEDURE FOR MAKING THE HULLS OF CABIN CRUISERS.

SIT ON MY LAP, CLIVE. I'LL SHOW YOU HOW IT WORKS!

CAN I DRIVE IT?

OF COURSE, AS LONG AS YOU LISTEN TO WHAT I TELL YOU!

1973

THE BRAZILIAN GP. LOTUS HAS SWITCHED FROM FIRESTONE TO GOODYEAR, WHICH HAS DEVELOPED INNOVATIVE NEW SLICK TYRES.

WHAT DO YOU THINK OF THESE NEW TYRES?

LIKE NIGHT AND DAY, JABBY... IN TESTING AT SILVERSTONE, EMERSON GAINED TWO AND A HALF SECONDS!

WITH PODIUM FINISHES TO HIS CREDIT AT MARCH, RONNIE PETERSON HAS JOINED TEAM LOTUS AS SECOND DRIVER. PETER WARR IS THE TEAM'S COMPETITION MANAGER.

PETERSON STRUGGLES WITH HIS ENGLISH AND SETTING UP THE CAR PROVES DIFFICULT FOR HIM.

COLIN, I JUST CAN'T DISCUSS ANYTHING WITH HIM. AND HE'S A SECOND SLOWER THAN FITTIPALDI.

GIVE HIM THE SAME SET-UP AS EMERSON!

ONE THING IS CLEAR: HE'S VERY QUICK, JUST LIKE CLARK AND RINDT.

WELL DONE, RONNIE! YOU'VE TAKEN POLE AHEAD OF EMERSON!

IN THE RACE, EMERSON WINS, WHILE RONNIE ENCOUNTERS MECHANICAL PROBLEMS.

THE SEASON HAS STARTED WELL FOR TEAM LOTUS.

THE 72E, DESIGNED FOR THE GOODYEAR TYRES, NOW REPLACES THE 72D. THE SAME SCENARIO IS REPEATED AT THE SPANISH GP: POLE FOLLOWED BY RETIREMENT FOR RONNIE, BUT A WIN FOR EMERSON.

FITTIPALDI CHALKS UP ANOTHER LANDMARK ACHIEVEMENT, LOTUS'S 50TH F1 WIN! PETERSON DROPS OUT WITH GEARBOX PROBLEMS.

PETERSON IS ACTUALLY QUICKER!

YES, BUT EMERSON ALREADY HAS THREE WINS, AND RONNIE HAS NO POINTS!

In June, production of the Lotus Seven ceases. Graham Nearn, a Lotus salesman since 1959, buys the Seven's name, plans and remaining stock.

The Super Seven will now be built under the Caterham name, after the town where Graham Nearn's premises are located.

Thanks for your trust in me, Colin...

Graham, I'm happy that the Seven is in good hands!

The Dutch GP. Between practice and the race, a number of drivers are down on the beach that borders the Zandvoort circuit.

Avec la mer du Nord ... pour dernier terrain vague..

Et des vagues de dunes... pour arrêter les vagues...

Bloody frogs!

* 'Le Plat Pays' (French song)

In the town where I was born, lived a man who sailed to sea*...

* 'Yellow Submarine' by the Beatles

Starting with the Dutch GP, Stewart scores 24 points in three races, while Fittipaldi gets only one and Peterson six.

MARTINI B

TEXACO FERODO

100

THEN COMES THE ITALIAN GP. RELATIONS BETWEEN FITTIPALDI AND PETERSON ARE TENSE. IN PRACTICE, RONNIE IS AGAIN ON POLE AND EMERSON IS FOURTH.

TO BEAT STEWART TO THE TITLE, YOU'VE GOT TO WIN THE LAST THREE RACES!

RONNIE HAS TO GIVE WAY TO ME... I'LL LEAVE IT TO YOU TO SORT IT OUT WITH HIM...

THE TWO LOTUSES ARE IN FRONT THROUGHOUT THE RACE.

VROOOOOO

FINALLY, PETERSON COMES OUT ON TOP, AHEAD OF HIS TEAM-MATE, PUTTING PAID TO EMERSON'S TITLE HOPES.

EMERSON IS FURIOUS THAT RONNIE IGNORED HIS BOSS'S ORDERS.

WHY DIDN'T YOU LET ME WIN?

I DIDN'T SIGNAL RONNIE TO LET YOU PASS...

STEWART WAS FOURTH AND THAT WAS ENOUGH FOR HIM TO TAKE THE TITLE.

CHAPMAN IS DELIGHTED WITH THE WIN, WHICH PUTS LOTUS WITHIN THREE POINTS OF TYRRELL IN THE CONSTRUCTORS' CHAMPIONSHIP.

AT WATKINS GLEN, F1 IS PLUNGED INTO MOURNING AFTER THE DEATH OF FRANÇOIS CEVERT DURING PRACTICE.

STEWART HAD ALREADY DECIDED TO RETIRE AND LEAVE HIS NUMBER ONE STATUS AT TYRRELL TO CEVERT.

TERRIBLE NEWS HERE. WE HAVE TRAGICALLY LOST THE DASHING FRANÇOIS CEVERT. AFTER ROGER WILLIAMSON, TWO MONTHS AGO...

THE NEXT DAY, PETERSON WINS AGAIN.

WELL DONE, RONNIE! THAT'S FANTASTIC!

TEAM LOTUS TAKES ITS SIXTH CONSTRUCTORS' CHAMPIONSHIP.

EMERSON, I'VE SUPPORTED YOU SINCE F3 DAYS. I GIVE YOU MY WORD THAT...

TOO LATE, I'VE ALREADY SIGNED FOR MCLAREN!

THAT'S RIDICULOUS; WE'VE WON TWO TITLES TOGETHER...

YES, TWO TITLES FOR THE TEAM, BUT ONLY ONE FOR ME!

LATE 1973...

IS THE 1974 SEASON ACTUALLY GOING TO HAPPEN?

FINANCIAL TIMES
OIL CRISIS
What is about to change as prices reach historic peak

OPEC ANNOUNCES A SIGNIFICANT RISE IN THE PRICE OF OIL AND AN EMBARGO ON CERTAIN COUNTRIES.

THEY'RE ALREADY CANCELLING A NUMBER OF RACES FOR 1974, BUT NOT IN F1...

8

1974

RALPH BELLAMY, FORMERLY OF McLAREN, HAS BEEN TASKED WITH WORKING ON A REPLACEMENT FOR THE 72, WHICH HAS BECOME TOO HEAVY.

I WANT A CAR THAT'S 50KG LIGHTER!

OK. YOU CAN RELY ON ME, COLIN...

JPS HAS RENEWED ITS CONTRACT WITH THE TEAM. PETERSON BECOMES THE NUMBER ONE DRIVER AND JACKY ICKX HAS LEFT FERRARI FOR TEAM LOTUS.

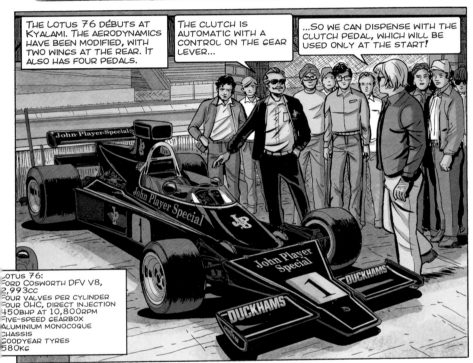

THE LOTUS 76 DÉBUTS AT KYALAMI. THE AERODYNAMICS HAVE BEEN MODIFIED, WITH TWO WINGS AT THE REAR. IT ALSO HAS FOUR PEDALS.

THE CLUTCH IS AUTOMATIC WITH A CONTROL ON THE GEAR LEVER...

...SO WE CAN DISPENSE WITH THE CLUTCH PEDAL, WHICH WILL BE USED ONLY AT THE START!

LOTUS 76:
FORD COSWORTH DFV V8, 2,993CC
FOUR VALVES PER CYLINDER
FOUR OHC, DIRECT INJECTION
450BHP AT 10,800RPM
FIVE-SPEED GEARBOX
ALUMINIUM MONOCOQUE CHASSIS
GOODYEAR TYRES
580KG

AND THANKS TO THE TWO BRAKE PEDALS, I'LL BE ABLE TO BRAKE WITH MY LEFT FOOT AS IN KARTING!

AT THE SOUTH AFRICAN, SPANISH AND BELGIAN GPs, THE 76 SEEMS UNDER-POWERED AND SUFFERS RELIABILITY PROBLEMS.

THE 72E CARS ARE DUSTED DOWN FOR THE MONACO GP. THE 76 WON'T BE SEEN AGAIN.

ROOOOOAA

PETERSON WINS AT MONACO, THEN IN FRANCE AND ITALY.

WHAT A LOT OF TIME AND MONEY WASTED...

AND TO CAP IT ALL, THE 76 WAS HEAVIER THAN THE 72E!

MEANWHILE, THE COMPETITION HASN'T BEEN WASTING ITS TIME. FITTIPALDI IN HIS McLAREN M23 TAKES THREE WINS.

REGAZZONI AND LAUDA IN THE FERRARI 312B3s ALSO HAVE THREE WINS.

SCHECKTER IN HIS TYRRELL 007 HAS TWO.

THE LOTUSES HAVE HAD TO RETIRE TOO OFTEN. FITTIPALDI WINS THE TITLE.

PETERSON IS FIFTH, ICKX TENTH.

WELL DONE, TEDDY!

THANKS, COLIN!

YOU'RE LUCKY TO HAVE FITTIPALDI TO WIN THE TITLE...

COLIN, YOU KEEP MAKING THE SAME MISTAKES!

TOO MANY INNOVATIONS, NOT ENOUGH RELIABILITY...

FORTUNATELY FOR US!

IN THE MIDDLE OF THE OIL CRISIS, WITH SPEED LIMITS IMPOSED, LOTUS LAUNCHES A NEW RANGE. IT REQUIRED SIGNIFICANT INVESTMENT AND IS AIMED AT A WEALTHIER AND SLIGHTLY OLDER CLIENTELE.

THIS CAR IS THE FIRST IN OUR NEW RANGE OF PRODUCTION MODELS...

THE NEW ELITE S2, A MORE LUXURIOUS CAR THAN OUR OLD ELAN +2.

IT'S A REAL FOUR-SEATER, WHICH PUTS IT FIRMLY IN THE GT MARKET.

LOTUS ELITE S2:
LOTUS 907 ENGINE PLACED LONGITUDINALLY AT THE FRONT
IN-LINE FOUR-CYLINDER, DOHC, 16 VALVES
1,973CC, 160BHP AT 6,200RPM
FIVE-SPEED GEARBOX,
REAR-WHEEL DRIVE
BACKBONE CHASSIS
POLYESTER COMPOSITE BODY
1160KG

A FEW MONTHS LATER, THE ECLAT APPEARS, A FASTBACK VERSION OF THE ELITE. ALTHOUGH PRESENTED AS A SPORTS CAR, IT IS RATHER LESS SPORTY THAN THE ELAN, WHICH HAS BEEN DROPPED.

LOTUS ECLAT:
LOTUS 907 FRONT-MOUNTED LONGITUDINAL ENGINE
IN-LINE FOUR-CYLINDER, DOHC, 16 VALVES
1,973CC, 160BHP AT 6,200RPM
FIVE-SPEED GEARBOX,
REAR-WHEEL DRIVE
BACKBONE CHASSIS
POLYESTER COMPOSITE BODY
1060KG

11

THE VACUUM-MOULDING PROCESS HAD BEEN DEVELOPED BY COLIN. ORIGINALLY INTENDED FOR BOAT HULLS, IT WAS ALSO USED IN MAKING BODIES FOR THE ELITE S2 AND THE ECLAT.

SO, TONY, HOW'S THE MOULDING GOING?

AFTER A FEW INITIAL PROBLEMS, IT'S NOW SPOT-ON!

THE ELITE S2 AND THE ECLAT HAVE A BACKBONE CHASSIS AND AN ALUMINIUM, 2-LITRE, 907 LOTUS ENGINE.

YOU'VE DONE A GREAT JOB ON THE ENGINE, WELL DONE...

HOWEVER, THE SELLING PRICE OF THE TWO CARS IS ABOVE WHAT HAD BEEN ENVISAGED, AND SALES ARE WELL BELOW EXPECTATIONS.

DECEMBER 1974, JPS HQ.

COLIN, I HAVE BAD NEWS...

IT LOOKS AS IF CIGARETTE ADVERTISING IS GOING TO BE BANNED...

TO KEEP A LOW PROFILE, JPS HAS DECIDED TO REDUCE ITS SPONSORSHIP.

WHAT!

SORRY, COLIN...

AND YOU'RE TELLING ME THIS JUST SIX WEEKS BEFORE THE FIRST GP!

WE REALISE WE'RE RATHER LATE INFORMING YOU.

AT LEAST GIVE ME SOME CHANCE TO KEEP MY TEAM GOING...

ALL RIGHT... WE'LL GIVE YOU 40% OF LAST YEAR'S BUDGET!

WHAT DO YOU SAY?

DO I HAVE TO SAY 'THANK YOU'?

IT'S CLEAR THAT 1975 IS GOING TO BE A TOUGH YEAR.

12

1975

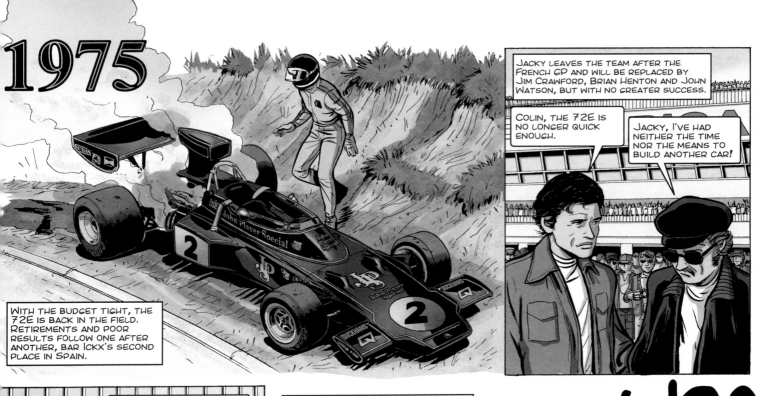

JACKY LEAVES THE TEAM AFTER THE FRENCH GP AND WILL BE REPLACED BY JIM CRAWFORD, BRIAN HENTON AND JOHN WATSON, BUT WITH NO GREATER SUCCESS.

COLIN, THE 72E IS NO LONGER QUICK ENOUGH.

JACKY, I'VE HAD NEITHER THE TIME NOR THE MEANS TO BUILD ANOTHER CAR!

WITH THE BUDGET TIGHT, THE 72E IS BACK IN THE FIELD. RETIREMENTS AND POOR RESULTS FOLLOW ONE AFTER ANOTHER, BAR ICKX'S SECOND PLACE IN SPAIN.

COME ON, COLIN, YOU'LL TURN THINGS AROUND.

I DO HOPE SO.

PETERSON AND ICKX ARE 13TH AND 16TH IN THE DRIVERS' CHAMPIONSHIP, DOMINATED BY LAUDA IN HIS FERRARI.

AS IN 1971, TEAM LOTUS DOESN'T WIN A SINGLE RACE AND ENDS UP ONLY SEVENTH IN THE CONSTRUCTORS' CHAMPIONSHIP!

WELL, GRAHAM, HOW ARE SALES OF THE NEW RANGE GOING?

WELL SHORT OF TARGET... BUT THE ECLAT IS DOING BETTER THAN THE ELITE.

THE PRODUCTION CARS ARE NOT DOING MUCH BETTER. FOR COLIN, WORN DOWN BY THE FINANCIAL PROBLEMS, THIS IS BECOMING A NIGHTMARE.

AND PROBLEMS WITH THE RELIABILITY OF OUR CARS DON'T HELP...

I'M FED UP WITH ALL THESE PROBLEMS, HAZEL.

CHEER UP, COLIN... YOU'LL GET THROUGH THEM.

13

A FEW DAYS LATER, WITH TONY RUDD AND PETER WRIGHT.

GENTLEMEN, WE DIDN'T INVENT ELECTRICITY BY REFINING THE CANDLE...

INSPIRED BY THE EVERYDAY SOUND OF A DOOR SLAMMING BEHIND HIM, COLIN SPENT MUCH OF HIS HOLIDAYS WORKING ON AERODYNAMICS.

BANG!

THAT SUMMER, IN IBIZA, I WAS SETTING OFF FOR THE BEACH WITH THE CHILDREN. THE HOUSE DOOR SLAMMED SHUT BEHIND ME...

FUII

THEN I HAD AN IDEA!

COULD YOU BE A LITTLE MORE PRECISE, COLIN?

THE VENTURI EFFECT, LOWERING OF PRESSURE... SEE WHAT I MEAN?

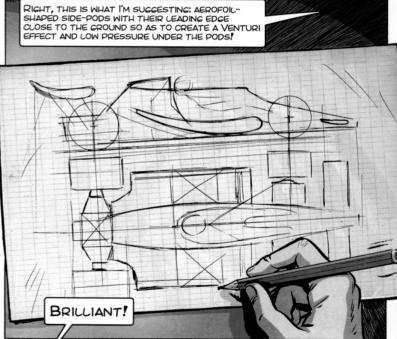

RIGHT, THIS IS WHAT I'M SUGGESTING: AEROFOIL-SHAPED SIDE-PODS WITH THEIR LEADING EDGE CLOSE TO THE GROUND SO AS TO CREATE A VENTURI EFFECT AND LOW PRESSURE UNDER THE PODS!

BRILLIANT!

SHORTLY AFTERWARDS, THE FIRST TESTS ARE HELD IN THE WIND TUNNEL AT IMPERIAL COLLEGE, LONDON, WITH A QUARTER-SCALE MODEL ON A ROLLING ROAD.

COLIN, LOOK!

THE ROAD IS LIFTING AND STICKING TO THE BASE OF THE MODEL!

JUST AS WE HOPED, THE LOWER PRESSURE UNDER THE SIDE-POD AEROFOILS IS SUCKING THE CAR DOWNWARDS!

FANTASTIC!

LOTUS HAS WORKED OUT HOW TO CREATE DOWNFORCE WITHOUT THE DRAG PROBLEM.

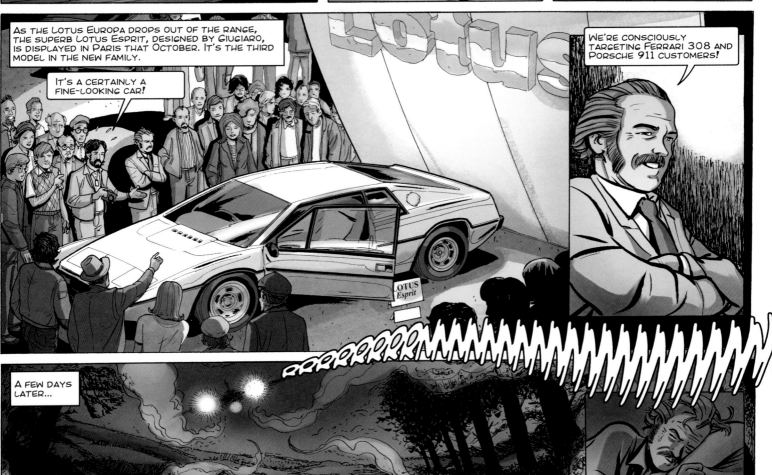

AS THE LOTUS EUROPA DROPS OUT OF THE RANGE, THE SUPERB LOTUS ESPRIT, DESIGNED BY GIUGIARO, IS DISPLAYED IN PARIS THAT OCTOBER. IT'S THE THIRD MODEL IN THE NEW FAMILY.

IT'S A CERTAINLY A FINE-LOOKING CAR!

WE'RE CONSCIOUSLY TARGETING FERRARI 308 AND PORSCHE 911 CUSTOMERS!

A FEW DAYS LATER...

RIIIING

COLIN, I'VE GOT SOME VERY BAD NEWS...

WHAT IS IT, JABBY?

GRAHAM HILL WAS KILLED TONIGHT, IN HIS PIPER, COMING BACK FROM LE CASTELLET. IT WAS FOGGY...

OH NO, IT CAN'T BE...

HILL WAS ONLY 46. HIS PILOT, TONY BRISE, AND FOUR OTHER PEOPLE ALSO DIED IN THE CRASH.

1976

WHILE WAITING FOR A GROUND-EFFECT CAR TO BE BUILT, COLIN HAS HAD THE IDEA OF MAKING A 'VARIABLE-GEOMETRY' CAR THAT WOULD ADAPT ITSELF TO THE CHARACTERISTICS OF EACH DIFFERENT CIRCUIT.

LOTUS 77 :
FORD COSWORTH DFV
V8 (90°), 2,993 CC
FOUR VALVES PER CYLINDER
DIRECT FUEL INJECTION
465BHP AT 10,800RPM
SIX-SPEED GEARBOX
ALUMINIUM MONOCOQUE CHASSIS
GOODYEAR TYRES
593KG

WITH THE ABILITY TO CHANGE SETTINGS AND COMPONENTS IN THE SUSPENSION AT BOTH FRONT AND REAR, WE CAN MAKE ALMOST INFINITE ADJUSTMENTS...

WITH GEOFF ALDRIDGE AND MARTIN OGILVIE, HE TRIED OUT THE CONCEPT ON THE NEW LOTUS 77.

WE CAN INCREASE OR REDUCE THE TRACK WIDTH AS NECESSARY.

AND WE'VE GOT ABOUT 10 INCHES TO PLAY WITH ON THE WHEELBASE...

LOTUS 77 1976
-Frames technology

ON THE FINANCIAL SIDE, JPS WAS NO MORE GENEROUS. COLIN HAD TO LET PETERSON GO TO MARCH. MARIO ANDRETTI IS BACK WITH TEAM LOTUS. HE IS PAID ACCORDING TO HOW MANY POINTS HE WINS.

I'M SO PLEASED TO BE JOINING SUCH A GREAT TEAM...

GUNNAR NILSSON, A YOUNG SWEDE WHO CAME TO PROMINENCE THROUGH HIS F3 SUCCESS, WILL BE THE SECOND DRIVER.

HOWEVER, THE 77 IS UNRELIABLE. WORSE, THE MULTIPLICITY OF ADJUSTMENT POSSIBILITIES, SUPPOSEDLY A BENEFIT, ULTIMATELY COMPLICATES THE JOB OF BOTH DRIVERS AND ENGINEERS.

I WANT A NARROWER FRONT TRACK WIDTH.

NO, NO, I THINK IT'S ALL RIGHT AS IT IS...

I SUGGEST YOU ADJUST THE WHEELBASE A BIT...

THE WHEELBASE?

THE SEASON WAS MARKED BY LAUDA'S DRAMATIC CRASH AT THE NÜRBURGRING, WHILE LEADING THE CHAMPIONSHIP. THERE WERE FEARS FOR HIS LIFE.

A FEW DAYS LATER, NILSSON IS SECRETLY TESTING THE BRAND-NEW 78 AT SNETTERTON.

WITHOUT THE DRIVERS' INTERVENTION, NIKI WOULD NEVER HAVE GOT OUT!

THAT'S TRUE, BOB, BUT THE NEWS IS NOT GOOD... A PRIEST HAS GIVEN HIM THE LAST RITES.

BROP...
BRÖÄW

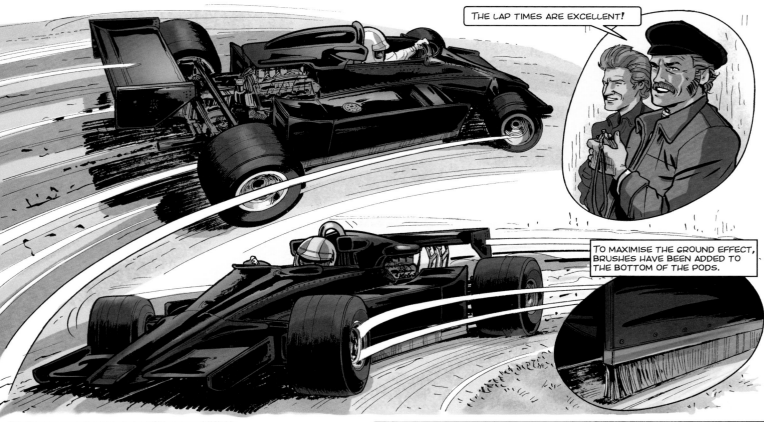

THE LAP TIMES ARE EXCELLENT!

TO MAXIMISE THE GROUND EFFECT, BRUSHES HAVE BEEN ADDED TO THE BOTTOM OF THE PODS.

THIS IS AN INCREDIBLE CAR. IT STICKS TO THE GROUND!

WE NEED TO KEEP THIS SECRET! WE WON'T BE RACING THIS CAR UNTIL NEXT SEASON!

THAT WAY, OUR COMPETITORS WON'T BE ABLE TO REACT OVER THE WINTER...

LAUDA IS BACK FOR THE ITALIAN GP, ONLY 39 DAYS AFTER HIS CRASH. HE AND HUNT ARE BATTLING IT OUT FOR THE TITLE.

SUCH COURAGE!

AN AMAZING GUY...

17

WHILE LAUDA FINISHES A HEROIC FOURTH AT MONZA AND THIRD AT WATKINS GLEN, HUNT WINS THE CANADIAN AND UNITED STATES GPs.

LAUDA IS STILL THREE POINTS AHEAD OF HUNT. EVERYTHING DEPENDS ON THE FINAL RACE AT MOUNT FUJI.

BY THE SECOND LAP, LAUDA HAS DECIDED TO RETIRE, JUDGING THE CONDITIONS TOO DANGEROUS TO CONTINUE.

AFTER WHAT HAPPENED, I CAN FULLY UNDERSTAND...

ME, TOO!

ANDRETTI WINS THE JAPANESE GP.

IT'S TEAM LOTUS'S ONLY WIN OF THE SEASON, AND HUNT, FINISHING IN THIRD PLACE, BECOMES THE WORLD CHAMPION.

AFTER THIS FURTHER MEDIOCRE SEASON, TEAM LOTUS FINISHES FOURTH IN THE CONSTRUCTORS' CHAMPIONSHIP, WELL BEHIND FERRARI, McLAREN AND TYRRELL.

IN THE MEANTIME, THE LOTUS GROUP IS BACK OUT OF THE RED, THANKS TO SALES OF THE ESPRIT.

WITH PETER WARR'S DEPARTURE, I INTEND TO DEVOTE MYSELF FULL-TIME TO THE RACING TEAM.

BUT THE FRUITFUL PARTNERSHIP WITH JENSEN-HEALEY HAS ENDED.

FRED, I WANT YOU TO RELEASE ME FROM ALL THE PROBLEMS OF THE LOTUS GROUP...

CERTAINLY, I'LL GET IT ORGANISED!

LET'S ALSO TRANSFER THE COMPETITION SIDE TO KETTERINGHAM HALL, SO I NO LONGER HAVE TO DEAL WITH THE FACTORY.

A GOOD IDEA! THAT WAY, YOU'LL HAVE THE WHOLE F1 TEAM AT HAND...

18

CHRISTMAS 1976 IS PARTICULARLY SAD. STAN CHAPMAN, COLIN'S FATHER, IS KILLED IN AN ACCIDENT ON HIS WAY TO BE WITH THE FAMILY.

I DIDN'T HAVE TIME TO TELL HIM HOW MUCH I ADMIRED HIM...

HE KNEW, COLIN!

IT'S A HEAVY BLOW FOR COLIN.

1977

THE SEASON NOW CONSISTS OF 17 GPs. AT LONG BEACH, ANDRETTI CLINCHES THE 78'S FIRST WIN. HE WINS AGAIN AT JARAMA. IT'S THE 60TH F1 VICTORY FOR A LOTUS.

LOTUS 78:
FORD COSWORTH DFV V8 ENGINE, 2,993CC
FOUR VALVES PER CYLINDER
FOUR OHC, DIRECT INJECTION
470BHP AT 11,000RPM
SIX-SPEED GEARBOX
ALUMINIUM MONOCOQUE CHASSIS
GOODYEAR TYRES
588KG

ON THE 78, THE NYLON BRUSHES HAVE BEEN REPLACED WITH POLYETHYLENE 'SKIRTS'.

AFTER 20 SEASONS IN F1, CHAPMAN IS ONCE AGAIN ON TOP.

COLIN, YOUR LOTUS CARS HAVE WON MORE RACES THAN ANY OTHER TEAM, SINCE YOUR FIRST GP.*

BUT THE BEST IS STILL TO COME, JABBY!

GUNNAR NILSSON FULFILS THE HOPES PLACED IN HIM BY WINNING AT ZOLDER. MARIO FOLLOWS UP WITH TWO MORE WINS, AT DIJON AND MONZA.

I'M VERY PLEASED WITH YOUR FIRST SEASON, GUNNAR.

* MONACO, 1958. IN THE SAME PERIOD FERRARI WON 41 RACES.

IN THE NEW JAMES BOND FILM 'THE SPY WHO LOVED ME', THE ESPRIT PLAYS A MAJOR ROLE, GIVING A BOOST TO LOTUS SALES.

IN THE ENSUING GPs, THE LOTUS 78 ENCOUNTERS TOO MANY RELIABILITY PROBLEMS. LAUDA TAKES WINS AND PODIUM PLACES ONE AFTER THE OTHER. HE TAKES HIS SECOND WORLD CHAMPIONSHIP TITLE AND GIVES FERRARI ITS FIFTH CONSTRUCTORS' TITLE.

WELL, THAT WAS ANOTHER FRUITLESS SEASON!

MANY RETIREMENTS...

YES, WE'VE GOT TO WORK ON THE 78'S RELIABILITY...

WE'VE GOT TO WIN BOTH CHAMPIONSHIPS NEXT YEAR...

YOU CAN RELY ON US...

COLIN, MARIO, I HAVE SOMETHING TO TELL YOU...

SADLY, DOCTORS HAVE DIAGNOSED GUNNAR WITH CANCER. HE WILL BE UNABLE TO RACE NEXT SEASON.

1978

After two seasons with March and Tyrrell, Peterson is back alongside Andretti. They start the season in the 78.

Patrick Depailler

Nationality	French
Team	Tyrrell
Points	23
Age	35

Mario Andretti

Nationality	American
Team	Lotus
Points	18
Age	38

Niki Lauda

Nationality	Austrian
Team	Brabham
Points	16
Age	29

After the first five GPs, there's a battle between five drivers.

Carlos Reutemann

Nationality	Argentine
Team	Ferrari
Points	18
Age	35

Ronnie Peterson

Nationality	Swedish
Team	Lotus
Points	14
Age	34

At Monaco, François Mazet introduces David Thieme to Chapman. Colin is captivated by this man.

François tells me that you made your money in oil...

Yes, that's right. I set up the Essex Company ten years ago.

David is passionate about F1. He'd like to help you...

Really?

The Lotus 79 appears at the Belgian GP at Zolder.

Is it different from the 78 to drive?

It's more efficient and easier to drive!

It's a development of the 78, with removable side-pods, so that the wings can be changed depending on the track. The first car is entrusted to Andretti.

Journalists have already dubbed it 'The Black Beauty'!

To fit the profile of the road surface, the 79's skirts now slide.

Lotus 79:
Ford Cosworth DFV V8 engine, 2,993cc
Four valves per cylinder
Four OHC, direct injection
475bhp at 11,000rpm
Six-speed gearbox
Aluminium monocoque chassis
Goodyear tyres
575kg

21

ANDRETTI WINS AND PETERSON COMES SECOND IN THE 78.

FOLLOWING THAT, ANDRETTI WINS IN SPAIN, FRANCE, GERMANY AND HOLLAND. PETERSON TAKES THE AUSTRIAN GP AND HAS THREE PODIUM PLACES.

DUTCH GI

BUT RONNIE IS TIRING OF THE ROLE OF SECOND DRIVER.

EVEN THOUGH THERE ARE STILL FOUR GPs TO GO, TEAM LOTUS IS ALREADY CELEBRATING ITS SEVENTH CONSTRUCTORS' CHAMPIONSHIP.

WHO ARE YOU LOOKING FOR?

OH, GUNNAR! IT'S GREAT TO SEE YOU!

WELL DONE ON THE TITLE, COLIN!

THANK YOU. WE MISS YOU, GUNNAR!

THE 79 REALLY IS A FANTASTIC CAR!

TRY IT WHENEVER YOU WANT...

PHOENIX AIRPORT, ARIZONA.

JOHN DELOREAN GOT IN TOUCH WITH ME RECENTLY TO TALK TO ME ABOUT HIS PLANS. HE WAS VICE-CHAIRMAN OF GENERAL MOTORS ONLY FOUR YEARS AGO!

HE'S LOOKING FOR A COMPANY CAPABLE OF AN AMBITIOUS PROJECT TO BUILD AN ULTRA-MODERN SPORTS CAR.

THAT FITS IN WELL WITH LOTUS ENGINEERING'S SKILLS.

HELLO, COLIN. MAY I INTRODUCE MY WIFE, CHRISTINA?

DELIGHTED TO MEET YOU! THIS IS MIKE KIMBERLEY, ONE OF OUR FINEST ENGINEERS...

AN ATTRACTIVE WOMAN, EH MIKE?

COLIN, MY DREAM HAS ALWAYS BEEN TO HAVE MY OWN CAR COMPANY! I ESTABLISHED THE DELOREAN MOTOR COMPANY THREE YEARS AGO AND WE'RE WORKING ON A CAR QUITE UNLIKE ANYTHING ELSE ON THE MARKET!

I WANT TO BUILD A REAR-ENGINED SPORTS CAR WITH STAINLESS-STEEL BODYWORK AND GULL-WING DOORS.

THIS IS THE PROTOTYPE OF THE FUTURE DMC-12! THE BODY DESIGN IS BY GIUGIARO AND THE TECHNICAL DESIGN WORK BY WILLIAM COLLINS, A FORMER GENERAL MOTORS ENGINEER.

THIS IS WILLIAM COLLINS. WE WANT TO FINALISE ALL ASPECTS OF THE CAR BEFORE GOING INTO PRODUCTION.

THE DISCUSSIONS GO WELL.

COMPOSITES FOR THE BODYWORK, A 2,850CC PRV V6 ENGINE... WE CAN BUILD IT UP ON A BACKBONE CHASSIS, WHICH IS ONE OF OUR SPECIALITIES...

AND OUR DESIGNERS COULD OFFER YOU A NUMBER OF OPTIONS.

COLIN, I'M SO PLEASED TO BE ABLE TO WORK WITH YOU...

23

THE 1978 SWEDISH GP IS A RARE OCCASION WHEN LOTUS LOSES OUT THAT YEAR. LAUDA, IN HIS REVOLUTIONARY BRABHAM BT46B, CRUSHES THE COMPETITION.

FOR ONCE, INNOVATION HASN'T COME FROM CHAPMAN. TO MAXIMISE THE GROUND EFFECT, ENGINEER GORDON MURRAY HAS INSTALLED A FAN THAT SUCKS UP AIR UNDER THE CAR TO LOWER THE PRESSURE.

IT IS INSPIRED BY THE CHAPARRAL 2J THAT APPEARED IN 1970. HOWEVER, IT IS ADJUDGED TO BE 'UNSAFE' AND THE TECHNOLOGY AND THE BRABHAM BT46B ARE BANNED A FEW DAYS LATER...

MONZA. THANKS TO A FURTHER ONE-TWO FROM ANDRETTI AND PETERSON IN HOLLAND, THEY ARE THE ONLY TWO DRIVERS IN THE RUNNING FOR THE TITLE. RONNIE IS JUST 12 POINTS BEHIND MARIO. ANDRETTI TAKES POLE AND PETERSON IS FIFTH ON THE GRID.

MARIO HAS A CHANCE OF WINNING THE RACE AND EVEN TAKING THE TITLE!

YOU KNOW THAT RONNIE'S ENGINE ISN'T RUNNING PROPERLY?

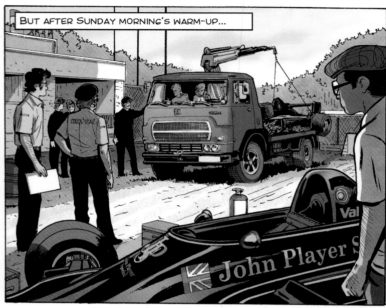

BUT AFTER SUNDAY MORNING'S WARM-UP...

I HAVE A BRAKE PROBLEM... I ENDED UP CRASHING.

MATHEMATICALLY, I CAN STILL BEAT MARIO TO THE CHAMPIONSHIP, BUT NOT WITHOUT A CAR!

COLIN, COULD I DRIVE MARIO'S SPARE IN THE RACE?

BUT CHAPMAN KNOWS THAT RONNIE HAS JUST SIGNED FOR McLAREN AS THEIR NUMBER ONE DRIVER FOR NEXT SEASON.

ON ONE CONDITION...

AS LONG AS YOU RENEW YOUR CONTRACT WITH US NEXT SEASON!

24

So Peterson has to make do with a 78 for the race. He's on the third row...

But there's chaos at the start.

The signal is given too early, before all the cars have stopped in their positions. Peterson, car 6, makes a poor start. Riccardo Patrese, starting from the middle of the grid in his Arrows, car 35, moves up on the right-hand side of the bunch...

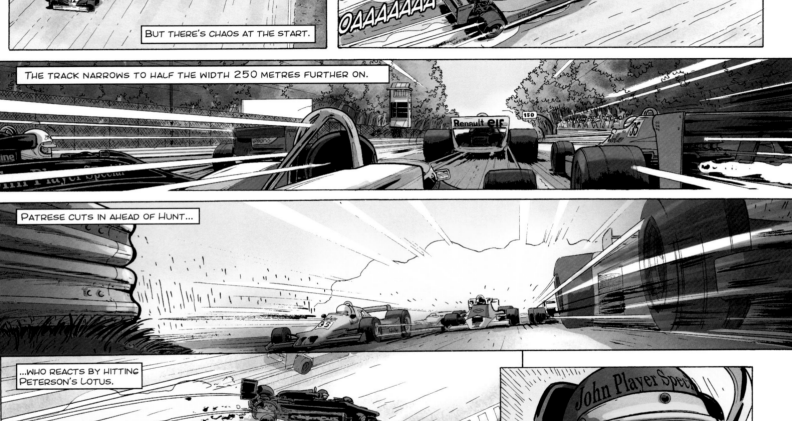

The track narrows to half the width 250 metres further on.

Patrese cuts in ahead of Hunt...

...who reacts by hitting Peterson's Lotus.

BANG

In the confusion, ten or so cars collide.

119

HUNT IS THE FIRST TO GET PETERSON OUT OF HIS LOTUS. HE IS CONSCIOUS, BUT HIS LEGS ARE BROKEN.

RONNIE, DON'T LOOK DOWN AT YOUR LEGS!

ANOTHER DRIVER, VITTORIO BRAMBILLA, IS INJURED. HE IS UNCONSCIOUS AND THE WORST IS FEARED FOR HIM.

POLICE STOP PROFESSOR SID WATKINS, HIRED BY BERNIE ECCLESTONE A FEW MONTHS BEFORE, GETTING THROUGH.

BUT I'M TELLING YOU I'M FORMULA 1'S CHIEF MEDICAL OFFICER!

IMPOSSIBLE!

AMID CHAOS, BRAMBILLA IS TAKEN AWAY.

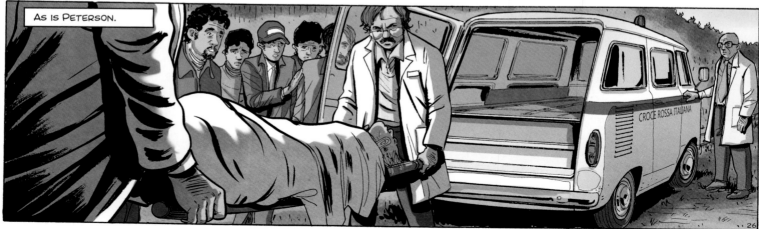

AS IS PETERSON.

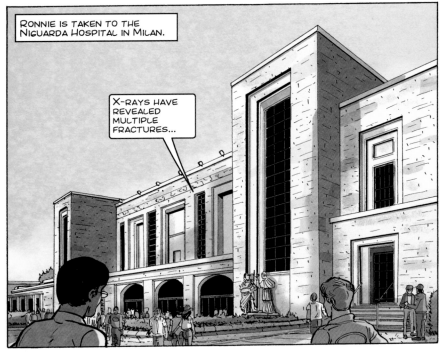

RONNIE IS TAKEN TO THE NIGUARDA HOSPITAL IN MILAN.

X-RAYS HAVE REVEALED MULTIPLE FRACTURES...

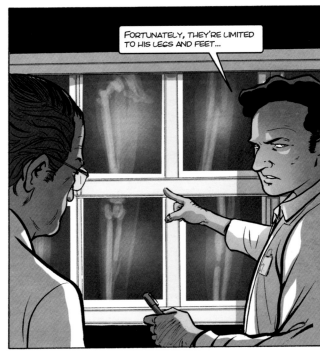

FORTUNATELY, THEY'RE LIMITED TO HIS LEGS AND FEET...

RONNIE ALSO HAS BURNS ON HIS LEFT ARM AND HAND. HE REMAINS CONSCIOUS.

WE MIGHT OPERATE TODAY?

I AGREE...

IN THE MEANTIME, THE RACE IS RE-STARTED. ANDRETTI COMES IN FIRST, BUT PICKS UP A ONE-MINUTE PENALTY FOR A FALSE START. HE'S FINALLY PLACED SIXTH.

ARE YOU PLEASED TO BE WORLD CHAMPION?

LEAVE ME ALONE... DO YOU THINK I WANT TO TALK ABOUT THAT NOW?

THE DOCTORS ARE OPTIMISTIC AND DECIDE TO OPERATE ON RONNIE IMMEDIATELY.

AND TWO AND A HALF HOURS LATER...

WE CAN CONFIDENTLY SAY THAT PETERSON WILL SOON BE WALKING AGAIN!

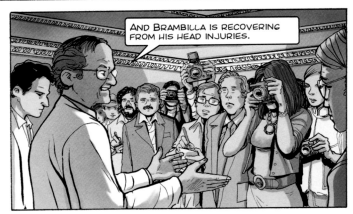

AND BRAMBILLA IS RECOVERING FROM HIS HEAD INJURIES.

AS RONNIE'S WIFE, BARBRO, ARRIVES IN MILAN DURING THE NIGHT, HIS CONDITION IS WORSENING.

HE FALLS INTO A COMA.

27

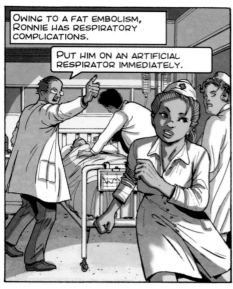

OWING TO A FAT EMBOLISM, RONNIE HAS RESPIRATORY COMPLICATIONS.

PUT HIM ON AN ARTIFICIAL RESPIRATOR IMMEDIATELY.

LOOK, THERE ARE CEREBRAL COMPLICATIONS.

OH GOD!

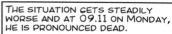

THE SITUATION GETS STEADILY WORSE AND AT 09.11 ON MONDAY, HE IS PRONOUNCED DEAD.

IT'S 1978 AND WE'RE SENDING ROCKETS INTO SPACE, YET THE DOCTORS STILL DON'T KNOW HOW TO DEAL WITH A SIMPLE EMBOLISM.

CALM DOWN, COLIN...

AWARE OF ITALIAN LAW, CHAPMAN HAS HAD PETERSON'S LOTUS SENT BACK TO ENGLAND BY THE SUNDAY EVENING.

John Player Team Lotus

DESPITE ANDRETTI BEING THE WORLD CHAMPION AND LOTUS HAVING WON THEIR SEVENTH CONSTRUCTORS' TITLE, COLIN IS DEEPLY SHAKEN.

PETERSON IS BURIED AT ÖREBRO, IN SWEDEN.

A MONTH LATER, A FURTHER TRAGEDY STRIKES: GUNNAR NILSSON DIES, AGED 29.

I'VE DECIDED TO SET UP A FOUNDATION TO FIGHT AGAINST CANCER... IT WILL BEAR THE NAME OF MY SON GUNNAR.

YOU CAN RELY ON MY SUPPORT.

MEANWHILE, CHAPMAN AND DELOREAN HAVE SIGNED A CONTRACT.

WE PLAN TO HAVE THE DMC-12 IN PRODUCTION WITHIN 12 MONTHS!

AS YOU CAN SEE, JOHN, WE'VE ALLOCATED 300 PEOPLE TO YOUR PROJECT...

FRED, I'M COUNTING ON YOU TO OVERSEE ALL THIS AND KEEP IT ON SCHEDULE...

OF COURSE, COLIN! I'VE SET UP EVERYTHING.

1979

THE SEASON BEGINS IN JANUARY, IN ARGENTINA, WITH THE PRICE OF OIL ROCKETING AGAIN.

GREEN LOTUSES?

MARTINI LOTUS

BACK TO 12 YEARS AGO!

YES, IT'S NICE. OUR NEW SPONSOR CHOSE IT.

CARLOS REUTEMANN HAS LEFT FERRARI TO JOIN ANDRETTI AT TEAM LOTUS.

SO, YOU'RE BACK HOME!

YES I LOVE THE ARGENTINE CROWDS; THEY'RE SO WARM AND ENTHUSIASTIC!

LOLE!

LOLE!

VIVA LOLE!

29

REUTEMANN FINISHES SECOND BEHIND LAFFITE. CLEARLY, DUCAROUGE, LIGIER'S TECHNICAL MANAGER, HAS MADE THE MOST OF GROUND EFFECT ON THE JS11.

A FEW MONTHS LATER, CHAPMAN TRIES OUT YET ANOTHER OF HIS REVOLUTIONARY IDEAS WITH THE 80: HE WILL OBTAIN ALL OF THE DOWNFORCE PURELY FROM GROUND EFFECT.

COLIN, WHAT'S YOUR AIM WITH THE 80?

SAME DOWNFORCE AS ON THE 79, BUT WITHOUT THE DRAG FROM WINGS. YOU SEE, EVEN THE NOSE HAS SKIRTS!

LOTUS 80:
FORD COSWORTH DFV V8 ENGINE, 2,993CC
FOUR VALVES PER CYLINDER
FOUR OHC, DIRECT INJECTION
475BHP AT 11,00RPM
FIVE-SPEED GEARBOX
ALUMINIUM MONOCOQUE CHASSIS
GOODYEAR TYRES
580KG

BUT FROM THE SPANISH GP, CONVENTIONAL WINGS APPEAR AT THE FRONT AND REAR OF THE 80, BECAUSE OF INSUFFICIENT DOWNFORCE... ANDRETTI FINISHES THIRD IN THE REVISED 80, BEHIND REUTEMANN IN THE 79!

ESSEX, DAVID THIEME'S COMPANY, IS TEAM LOTUS'S SECOND SPONSOR, A USEFUL FILLIP TO THE TEAM'S FINANCES.

AFTER THREE GRANDS PRIX, THE 80 IS STILL NOT UP TO EXPECTATIONS.

IT STILL HANDLES LIKE A PORPOISE. IT'S IMPOSSIBLE TO DRIVE...

WELL, IT'S NOT THROUGH LACK OF TRYING DIFFERENT SET-UPS!

WHILE THE FERRARI, WILLIAMS AND LIGIER ENGINEERS HAVE BUILT GROUND EFFECT INTO THEIR CARS, ANDRETTI HAS TO GO BACK TO THE 79 FOR THE NEXT GP.

AS EVER, CHAPMAN WANTS TO REVOLUTIONISE F1...

RATHER THAN TAKING THE TIME TO MAKE HIS CARS RELIABLE.

IF HE DID, LOTUS WOULD BE WORLD CHAMPIONS EVERY SEASON...

VROOAP
VROO

AS FERRARI AND SCHECKTER TAKE THEIR TITLES, LOTUS ENDS THE 1979 SEASON IN FOURTH PLACE, WITHOUT A SINGLE WIN.

30

MEANWHILE GROUP LOTUS'S SALES OF ROAD CARS ARE WELL SHORT OF THE TARGETS.

LOTUS ESPRIT S2:
LOTUS 910 ENGINE AMIDSHIPS
FOUR-CYLINDER IN LINE, DOHC, 16 VALVES
2,174CC, GARRETT T3 TURBO
210BHP AT 6,000RPM
FIVE-SPEED GEARBOX, REAR-WHEEL DRIVE
BACKBONE CHASSIS
POLYESTER COMPOSITE BODYWORK
1,270KG

I'M HOPING THE NEW VERSIONS OF THE ESPRIT WILL BOOST SALES.

I'M COUNTING ON THAT, BUT THERE'S ALSO YET ANOTHER HIKE IN OIL PRICES.

THE LOTUS ESPRIT SERIES 2 IS OFFERED WITH TWO ENGINE OPTIONS: NORMALLY ASPIRATED AND TURBOCHARGED.

TALBOT HAS ENTRUSTED LOTUS ENGINEERING WITH DEVELOPMENT AND PRODUCTION OF THE SUNBEAM-LOTUS.

THIS CONTRACT FORMS 40 PER CENT OF THE GROUP'S TURNOVER!

JUST AS WELL WE'VE GOT YOU, FRED...

THE HOT VERSION OF THE HUMBLE SUNBEAM, WITH A 2.2-LITRE LOTUS ENGINE, IS DESTINED TO GIVE TALBOT A SPORTING IMAGE.

TWO YEARS LATER, IT WOULD WIN THE WORLD RALLY CHAMPIONSHIP, THANKS, ESPECIALLY, TO GUY FRÉQUELIN AND JEAN TODT.

IN 1970, COLIN HAD BEEN AWARDED THE CBE (COMMANDER OF THE ORDER OF THE BRITISH EMPIRE) BY HER MAJESTY THE QUEEN.

I SEE THAT YOU ARE APPRECIATED IN HIGH PLACES, COLIN!

WITH ABOUT £50 MILLION* OF GOVERNMENT SUPPORT, DELOREAN BUILDS AN ULTRA-MODERN PLANT AT DUNMURRY, ON THE OUTSKIRTS OF BELFAST. BUT CONSTRUCTION SUFFERS DELAYS AND THE DMC-12'S SCHEDULE SLIPS AS A RESULT.

* EQUIVALENT TO ABOUT £230 MILLION IN 2013.

31

1980

Following tests with a variety of young drivers, Team Lotus signs Elio de Angelis alongside Mario Andretti. He is a highly talented driver, as well as being an excellent pianist!

Essex organises the launch of the 81 with great pomp at the Paradis Latin, in Paris.

Chapman and Ogilvie have quickly designed the 81 based on the shell of the 80 and with bodywork inspired by the 79.

Lotus 81:
Ford Cosworth DFV V8 engine, 2,993cc
Four valves per cylinder
Four OHC, direct injection
475bhp at 11,000rpm
Six-speed gearbox
Aluminium monocoque chassis
Goodyear tyres
590kg

But, apart from a second place from de Angelis in Brazil, the 1980 season proves to be a terrible one as a result of poor performance, technical problems and crashes.

ROOAAAAW

While Williams is the Constructors' Champion for the first time, thanks to Jones and Reutemann, Team Lotus finishes fifth without any wins for the second consecutive year.

Andretti has taken just one point from 14 races.

Mario, I'm sorry I haven't been able to give you the equipment you deserve...

Mario has decided to go to Alfa Romeo, which is making its big return to F1.

Let's forget that, Colin, and remember our 1978 titles!

32

126

COLIN DECIDES TO FINISH WITH HIS BOAT BUSINESSES, WHICH ARE LOSING MONEY. HIS MORALE IS AT A LOW EBB.

FOR A CHANGE OF SCENE, HE GETS INVOLVED IN MAKING MICROLIGHTS FROM COMPOSITE MATERIALS. HIS DAUGHTER, JANE, HELPS WITH THE TRIALS.

ARE YOU READY, JANE?

A WAR HAS BROKEN OUT BETWEEN FISA AND FOCA* AT THE 1980 SPANISH GP. FOCA WANTS CONTROL OF F1'S INCOME AND TECHNICAL DEVELOPMENT.

TWO-THIRDS OF THE FIELD USES THE COSWORTH ENGINE... THE TURBO WILL KILL F1!

HENCEFORTH, FOCA WILL CONTROL THE TECHNICAL REGULATIONS AND THE TV RIGHTS!

ONLY THE BIG MANUFACTURERS HAVE THE MEANS TO BUILD A TURBO ENGINE MORE POWERFUL THAN THE WELL-ESTABLISHED, NORMALLY ASPIRATED FORD COSWORTH.

JEAN-MARIE BALESTRE, FISA PRESIDENT, IS HAVING NONE OF IT.

OUT OF THE QUESTION! IT'S FISA'S JOB TO ADMINISTER F1'S REVENUES...

AS A MEMBER OF FISA'S TECHNICAL COMMISSION, CROMBAC IS OFFICIALLY IN THE OPPOSING CAMP TO CHAPMAN; AN AWKWARD POSITION.

THE TECHNICAL RULES ARE ALSO FISA'S RESPONSIBILITY!

IF YOU TURN US DOWN, WE'LL ORGANISE OUR OWN CHAMPIONSHIPS...

I'D LIKE TO SEE YOU TRY!

THE BATTLE IS AT ITS HEIGHT OVER THE WINTER OF 1980-81. FOCA SETS UP ITS OWN FEDERATION, THE WFMS. CHAPMAN IS GIVEN THE TASK OF DRAWING UP THE TECHNICAL REGULATIONS.

CAN YOU SHOW ME THE CLAUSES RELATING TO SUPERCHARGING AND SKIRTS?

YES, HERE IT IS: TURBOS BANNED AND SLIDING SKIRTS PERMITTED!

*FISA: FÉDÉRATION INTERNATIONALE DU SPORT AUTOMOBILE, CHAIRED BY JEAN-MARIE BALESTRE AND SUPPORTED BY THE BIG FACTORY TEAMS: FERRARI, RENAULT, ALFA ROMEO.
FOCA: FORMULA ONE CONSTRUCTORS ASSOCIATION, CHAIRED BY BERNIE ECCLESTONE, COMPOSED OF TEAMS OTHER THAN THE 'MANUFACTURER' TEAMS.

33

1981

On 7 February, the WFMS organises a South African GP at Kyalami. All the teams are there apart from, of course, the 'manufacturer' teams and Talbot-Ligier.

We've got 19 cars, all using Cosworth engines.

Balestre will get the message...

The balance of power is clearly in our favour!

Perhaps FISA will count this race?

No chance, Frank.

Reutemann wins in his Williams. But, of course, the results are not recognised by FISA.

After this show of strength, FISA and FOCA face up to the evidence: holding two competing championships will soon kill off F1.

So we are in agreement! The rules are to be those drawn up by FISA!

After the negotiations, the Concorde Agreement is signed in March. Sliding skirts are banned and turbos are sanctioned.

FOCA is assigned all TV rights and the task of selling the F1 package to the track owners.

Count on me to look after F1's best interests!

Meanwhile, production of the DMC-12 has finally started. The first customers will soon have their new cars.

34

128

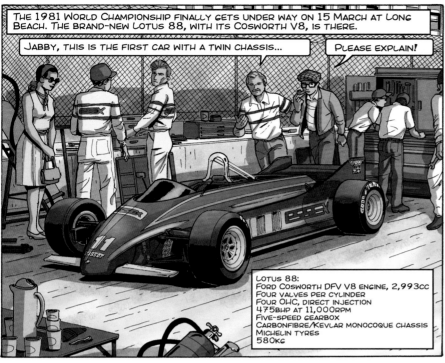

THE 1981 WORLD CHAMPIONSHIP FINALLY GETS UNDER WAY ON 15 MARCH AT LONG BEACH. THE BRAND-NEW LOTUS 88, WITH ITS COSWORTH V8, IS THERE.

JABBY, THIS IS THE FIRST CAR WITH A TWIN CHASSIS...

PLEASE EXPLAIN!

LOTUS 88:
FORD COSWORTH DFV V8 ENGINE, 2,993CC
FOUR VALVES PER CYLINDER
FOUR OHC, DIRECT INJECTION
475BHP AT 11,000RPM
FIVE-SPEED GEARBOX
CARBONFIBRE/KEVLAR MONOCOQUE CHASSIS
MICHELIN TYRES
580KG

WITH SKIRTS DOWN TO GROUND LEVEL BANNED, GROUND EFFECT IS MORE OR LESS NON-EXISTENT. BUT WRIGHT, OGILVIE AND CHAPMAN HAVE FOUND AN ANSWER. THE NEW 88 HAS TWO CHASSIS LINKED BY SPRINGS, GIVING THE DRIVER A DEGREE OF COMFORT.

IT'S VERY SIMPLE...

THE PRIMARY CHASSIS SUPPORTS THE BODY, SIDE-PODS AND HAS QUITE STIFF SUSPENSION...

THE SECONDARY, MONOCOQUE CHASSIS IS FOR THE DRIVER, ENGINE AND RUNNING GEAR.

NOTE THAT, FOR THE FIRST TIME, THESE TWO CHASSIS ARE MADE OUT OF KEVLAR AND CARBONFIBRE BY LOTUS THEMSELVES.

PRIMARY CHASSIS

SECONDARY CHASSIS

AS YOU CAN SEE, THE SKIRTS DESCEND TO GROUND LEVEL WHEN THE CAR IS ON THE MOVE!

COLIN, IN TWO WORDS, YOU'RE BRILLIANT AND INCORRIGIBLE!

CROMBAC IS VISIBLY TORN BETWEEN HIS ADMIRATION FOR CHAPMAN AND HIS ROLE ON FISA'S TECHNICAL COMMISSION.

I HOPE FISA AND YOUR COMPETITORS WILL SWALLOW IT!

FISA'S TECHNICAL INSPECTORS SPEND A LOT OF TIME GOING OVER THE 88.

35

HAVING BEEN OVER IT WITH A FINE TOOTHCOMB, I DECLARE YOUR CAR TO BE LEGAL.

I'M DELIGHTED TO HEAR IT!

DE ANGELIS BARELY HAS TIME TO COMPLETE A FEW PRACTICE LAPS WHEN THE TRACK STEWARDS FLAG HIM TO COME IN IMMEDIATELY.

TWELVE OF THE 16 TEAMS HAVE LODGED COMPLAINTS AGAINST THE 88. THE COMPETITION COMMITTEE PREPARES TO GIVE A RULING ON THE MATTER.

ELIO, TAKE THE 81B...

OK, I SUPPOSE WE HAD THAT COMING TO US!

LISTEN, GENTLEMEN, THAT CAR DOES NOT CONFORM TO THE SPIRIT OF THE RULES!

IF THE 88 IS ADJUDGED TO BE LEGAL, THREE-QUARTERS OF THE TEAMS WILL PULL OUT!

WE FULLY UNDERSTAND YOUR POINT OF VIEW...

UNDER PRESSURE FROM FISA AND MANY OF THE MANUFACTURERS, THE VERDICT IS DELIVERED.

MR CHAPMAN, OUR DECISION IS THAT THE 88 IS ILLEGAL!

THIS IS TOO MUCH FOR ME. I'M REALLY CHEESED OFF.

WE MUST FIND A GOOD LAWYER, QUICKLY...

CHAPMAN APPEALS AGAINST THE VERDICT TO ACCUS, THE AMERICAN FEDERATION.

OUR TRIBUNAL RULES THAT THIS CAR IS FULLY COMPLIANT WITH THE REGULATIONS!

36

After the race, Hinerfeld has taken the testimony of one of the Brazilian federation's scrutineers, who claims that the chairman of the federation offered him a job as long as he 'voted the right way' at the stewards' meeting!

That'll work in our favour!

Absolutely.

But in Argentina, the technical scrutineers record a negative verdict. For the third time, the 88 is forbidden from taking part in practice.

'The committee has adjudged the 88 to be illegal. But it wishes to express its admiration for the creative inventiveness of those who designed it.'

What a spineless bunch!

Exasperated, Chapman leaves Buenos Aires on Saturday. For the first time in 22 years, he is absent from a Grand Prix.

Colin takes advantage of the fact to witness the launch of Columbia, the very first space shuttle.

Rather than building a completely new rocket for each launch, NASA will now be able to re-use the shuttle time and again.

Hazel, that's a major technical leap...

I can understand the frustration you feel, Colin. There are so many conflicting interests in F1... Everyone fights his own corner.

F1 should be open to innovation. If we're not careful, it'll eventually be regulated down to the last bolt!

38

THE ARGENTINE GP IS WON BY PIQUET. HIS TEAM-MATE, REBAQUE, ABANDONS HIS BRABHAM ON THE TRACK IN ITS LOWERED POSITION. THE DECEPTION IS OBVIOUS.

JOHNNY, WILLIAMS'S COMPLAINT HAS BEEN REJECTED!

CAN YOU JUST REMIND ME WHO RUNS THE BRABHAM TEAM?

GOOD OLD BERNIE ECCLESTONE!

MEANWHILE, ESSEX IS IN GREAT FINANCIAL DIFFICULTY. THEIR LAWYER HAS COME TO ASK FOR HELP.

DAVID THIEME HAS BEEN TAKEN TO COURT BY A SWISS BANK. HE'S IN PRISON!

OK, I'LL PAY THE BAIL TO FREE HIM! HOW MUCH WILL IT BE?

THINGS ARE HARDLY ANY BETTER WITH DELOREAN. THE SALES FIGURES ARE A LONG WAY SHORT OF JOHN DELOREAN'S AMBITIOUS TARGETS. THE BRITISH GOVERNMENT HAS INVESTED A FURTHER £40 MILLION*...

SALES FOR THE YEAR ARE STALLED AT 6,000 CARS.

PROBLEMS ARE INCREASING. MEDICATION DOES LITTLE TO RELIEVE THE TIREDNESS AND STRESS COLIN IS SUFFERING.

WE'RE A LONG WAY FROM THE 20,000 CARS WE WANTED!

* THE EQUIVALENT OF NEARLY £163 MILLION IN 2013.

FINALLY, THE RESULT OF TEAM LOTUS'S APPEAL TO THE FIA.

THE APPEAL TRIBUNAL OF THE FIA HAS ADJUDGED THE LOTUS 88 TO BE...

...ILLEGAL!

THE FIA'S ARGUMENTS DO NOT EVEN RELY ON THE TECHNICAL RULES APPENDED TO THE CONCORDE AGREEMENT, BUT ON AN ARTICLE APPLICABLE TO TOURING CARS!

COLIN, THIS IS PURELY POLITICAL. I DID WARN YOU...

BALESTRE IS PAYING YOU BACK FOR YOUR ROLE AS A DISSIDENT IN THE WFMS!

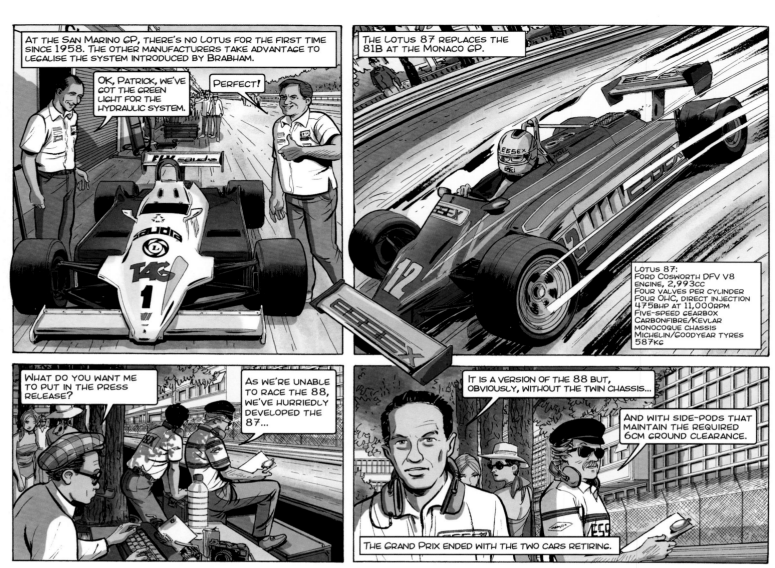

At the San Marino GP, there's no Lotus for the first time since 1958. The other manufacturers take advantage to legalise the system introduced by Brabham.

OK, PATRICK, WE'VE GOT THE GREEN LIGHT FOR THE HYDRAULIC SYSTEM.

PERFECT!

The Lotus 87 replaces the 81B at the Monaco GP.

LOTUS 87:
FORD COSWORTH DFV V8 ENGINE, 2,993CC
FOUR VALVES PER CYLINDER
FOUR OHC, DIRECT INJECTION
475BHP AT 11,000RPM
FIVE-SPEED GEARBOX
CARBONFIBRE/KEVLAR MONOCOQUE CHASSIS
MICHELIN/GOODYEAR TYRES
587KG

WHAT DO YOU WANT ME TO PUT IN THE PRESS RELEASE?

AS WE'RE UNABLE TO RACE THE 88, WE'VE HURRIEDLY DEVELOPED THE 87...

IT IS A VERSION OF THE 88 BUT, OBVIOUSLY, WITHOUT THE TWIN CHASSIS...

AND WITH SIDE-PODS THAT MAINTAIN THE REQUIRED 6CM GROUND CLEARANCE.

The Grand Prix ended with the two cars retiring.

Crombac was disciplined by FISA for his part in the case of the 88. He is no longer the chairman of the technical commission of the FFSA.*

TIP - TOP

SOME PEOPLE THINK THAT I'VE DONE TOO MUCH BEHIND THE SCENES FOR LOTUS...

TIP - TOP

TIP-TOP

Plat du Jour
* Magret de Canard
Endives Braisées et haricots verts.
Tarte au Citron. *

BALESTRE HAD IT IN FOR YOU!

DON'T WORRY, I'LL GET OVER IT...

I'M SORRY, JABBY... HERE, TAKE MY LOTUS ECLAT! I KNOW IT'S NOT MUCH CONSOLATION...

From the next Grand Prix, Team Lotus's cars are back in their black and gold livery. Essex remains as a joint sponsor.

LOOK, COLIN, WE'RE READY TO BE YOUR SPONSOR AGAIN FOR THE NEXT TWO YEARS...

THAT'S GREAT! OUR CARS WILL BE IN YOUR COLOURS AT THE SPANISH GP.

* FÉDÉRATION FRANÇAISE DU SPORT AUTOMOBILE.

40

AT THE FRENCH GP, THE YOUNG ALAIN PROST TAKES HIS FIRST F1 VICTORY IN THE POWERFUL RENAULT V6 TURBO.

DE ANGELIS AND MANSELL CAN DO NO BETTER THAN SIXTH AND SEVENTH PLACES, A LAP BEHIND PROST... THE 87 IS CLEARLY LACKING IN POWER.

FOR THE BRITISH GP, CHAPMAN DECIDES TO RACE THE 88. FOLLOWING A FAVOURABLE OPINION FROM THE BRITISH SCRUTINEERS, DE ANGELIS IS TO DRIVE IT IN PRACTICE.

YOU HOPE FISA WILL GIVE WAY AGAIN?

I'M COUNTING ON THE SUPPORT OF OUR SCRUTINEERS TO LET IT RACE!

BUT FOLLOWING A PROTEST FROM THE FACTORY TEAMS, THE BRITISH SCRUTINEERS, WHO ARE UNDER PRESSURE FROM FISA, DECLARE THE 88 ILLEGAL.

FISA WILL NEVER GO BACK ON ITS JUDGMENT, EVEN IF, BASICALLY, THE 88 DOES CONFORM TO THE REGULATIONS...

IT'S ALL A CONSPIRACY!

FOR HEAVEN'S SAKE, COLIN, JUST FORGET THE 88...

TEAM LOTUS FINISHES A DISAPPOINTING SEVENTH IN THE CONSTRUCTORS' CHAMPIONSHIP, WHICH IS WON BY WILLIAMS, AHEAD OF BRABHAM.

NOT A SINGLE WIN THIS YEAR, AND POOR RESULTS FOR THE LOTUS GROUP...

AND DAVID THIEME AND JOHN DELOREAN HAVE LEFT ME WITH A LOT OF UNPAID BILLS!

WHAT A BUSINESS, HAZEL!

1982
THE DELOREAN MOTOR COMPANY SUFFERS HUGE LOSSES, THANKS TO OVER-RUNNING COSTS AND VERY WEAK SALES. IN FEBRUARY, THE COMPANY GOES INTO RECEIVERSHIP.

IT WILL HAVE BEEN A COSTLY ADVENTURE FOR US, COLIN.

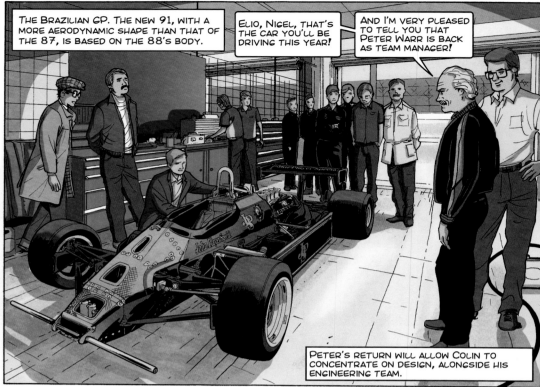

THE BRAZILIAN GP. THE NEW 91, WITH A MORE AERODYNAMIC SHAPE THAN THAT OF THE 87, IS BASED ON THE 88'S BODY.

ELIO, NIGEL, THAT'S THE CAR YOU'LL BE DRIVING THIS YEAR!

AND I'M VERY PLEASED TO TELL YOU THAT PETER WARR IS BACK AS TEAM MANAGER!

PETER'S RETURN WILL ALLOW COLIN TO CONCENTRATE ON DESIGN, ALONGSIDE HIS ENGINEERING TEAM.

BUT IS HIS HEART STILL IN IT?

I DON'T COLIN HAS THE SAME ENTHUSIASM ANY MORE.

IT'S JUST TEMPORARY. HE'LL SOON GET OVER THE 88 SAGA...

FRENCH GP, LE CASTELLET.

I JUST DON'T HAVE THE TOP SPEED!

YOUR V8 CAN'T COMPETE WITH THE TURBOS, ELIO...

THE TURBOCHARGED FERRARIS, RENAULTS AND BRABHAMS HAVE A STRING OF WINS AND PODIUM PLACES. LOTUS AND THE OTHER TEAMS HAVE TO MAKE DO WITH THE 'CRUMBS'. THE DIFFERENCE IN POWER BETWEEN THE TURBOS AND THE NORMALLY ASPIRATED ENGINES IS SUBSTANTIAL.

42

LAUDA IS NINTH IN PRACTICE. HE'S THE FASTEST OF THE COSWORTHS!

BUT HE'S STILL 3.3SEC BEHIND ARNOUX'S POLE...

THE AUSTRIAN GP. THE F1 PADDOCK AND THE CROWD ARE IN SHOCK AFTER THE SERIOUS ACCIDENT THAT BEFELL PIRONI, WHO WAS LEADING THE CHAMPIONSHIP, THE PREVIOUS WEEK AT HOCKENHEIM.

HE NEARLY HAD TO HAVE HIS LEGS AMPUTATED...

SUCH AWFUL NEWS, ALONG WITH VILLENEUVE'S DEATH AT ZOLDER.

FORTUNATELY, TAMBAY WAS THERE TO WIN AT HOCKENHEIM.

AT THE END OF AN ACTION-PACKED RACE, DE ANGELIS WINS, A MERE 0.125SEC AHEAD OF ROSBERG! IT'S TEAM LOTUS'S FIRST WIN IN FOUR YEARS!

VROAAAAMMMMOOOM

LOTUS'S 72ND WIN HAS COME AT JUST THE RIGHT TIME. COLIN IS DELIGHTED.

IT'S ALSO ELIO DE ANGELIS'S FIRST VICTORY. AND THE FORD COSWORTH ENGINE'S 150TH WIN SINCE 1967!

THE SEASON FINISHES AT LAS VEGAS. TEAM LOTUS IS FIFTH IN A CONSTRUCTORS' CHAMPIONSHIP WON BY FERRARI. ROSBERG WINS THE DRIVERS' TITLE.

THE FORTHCOMING 93T FOR 1983 WILL HAVE THE POWERFUL, TURBOCHARGED, 1,500CC RENAULT V6 ENGINE.

PERHAPS BETTER DAYS ARE ON THE WAY.

COLIN, YOU'RE PENSIVE...

I'M PLEASED TO HAVE SIGNED WITH RENAULT! IT'S THE ONLY WAY TO GET BACK ON THE WINNING TRACK.

YES, THE COSWORTH HAS BEEN TRAILING FOR SOME TIME...

ON THE WAY BACK FROM LAS VEGAS, COLIN DISCOVERS THAT THE BRITISH PRESS IS HAVING A FIELD DAY WITH THE DELOREAN AFFAIR.

LISTEN TO THIS, COLIN: 'DMC IS CLOSING LEAVING 2,600 PEOPLE OUT OF A JOB!'

AND 350 CREDITORS UNPAID.

THE UK GOVERNMENT HAS SET UP AN INQUIRY.

$240 MILLION HAS DISAPPEARED IN JOHN DELOREAN'S VARIOUS SUBSIDIARY COMPANIES...

WHAT A CROOK!

THAT MUCH MONEY HASN'T GONE MISSING SINCE THE GREAT TRAIN ROBBERY...

TAXPAYERS' MONEY TOTALLY DOWN THE DRAIN!

ON 19 OCTOBER, JOHN DELOREAN IS CHARGED WITH SMUGGLING COCAINE TO THE VALUE OF $24 MILLION.

HE HAS BEEN ARRESTED BY THE FBI IN LOS ANGELES ON DRUG-TRAFFICKING CHARGES.

WHAT A STORY!

I SIMPLY CAN'T BELIEVE IT!

IT'S THE FINAL BLOW FOR COLIN.

FRED, HAVE YOU SEEN THE TV?

YES, THAT'S IT FOR DMC...

IT'S TERRIBLE... WE DIDN'T NEED THIS, ON TOP OF EVERYTHING ELSE!

THE LOTUS GROUP, ALREADY SUFFERING FROM FINANCIAL PROBLEMS, HAS RECENTLY HAD TO BORROW MONEY.

COLIN IS UNABLE TO SLEEP. HE IS EXHAUSTED. HAZEL IS WORRIED.

44

On 14 December, Colin, Peter Warr and their wives go to listen to the jazz band of their friend, Chris Barber.

Early the next morning, Colin flies out to Paris with Fred Bushell and Jabby for a long and stormy meeting with FISA at the Place de la Concorde.

It's late in the evening when they get back to the company plane at Le Bourget. Colin is exhausted.

Sir, I'm sorry, but the side winds at Hethel are much stronger than normal; we're going to have to divert to another airport...

Oh no!

It's my plane, my company and my landing strip. Let me take over the controls. I'll land it myself!

Colin succeeds in landing the plane, despite the conditions.

Finally back at East Carleton, he goes to bed, feeling dizzy...

Around 5 o'clock in the morning, Colin succumbs to a massive heart attack.

45

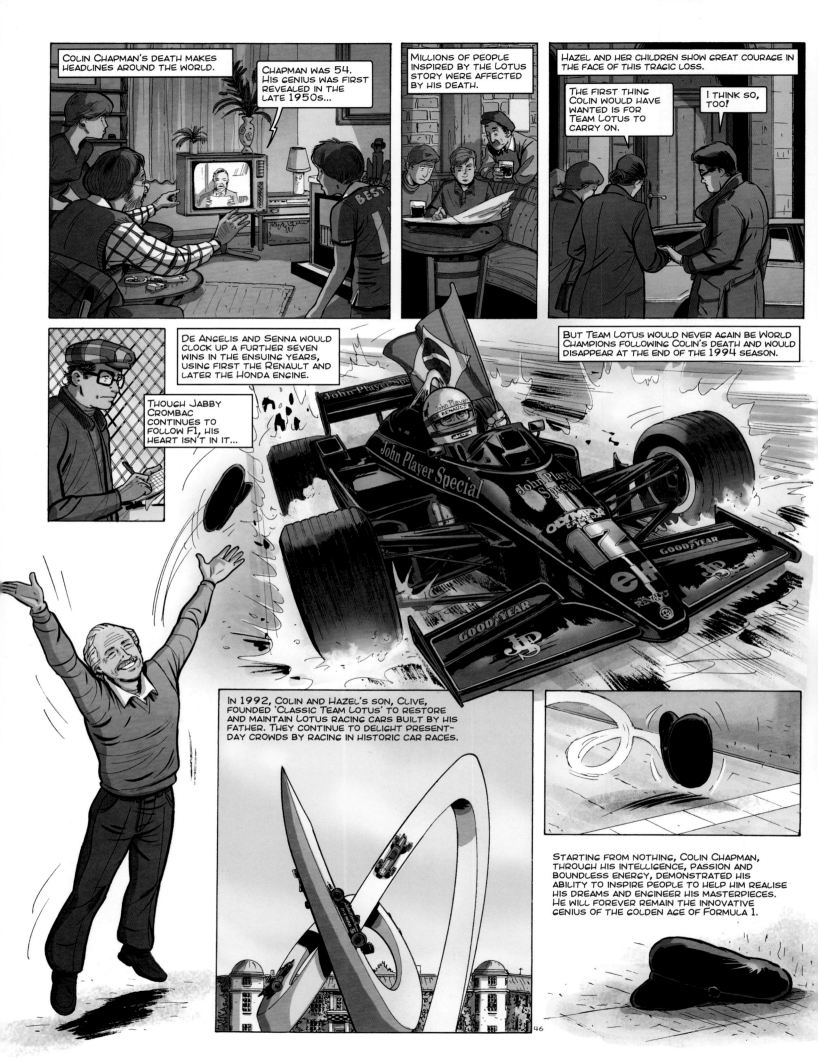

COLIN CHAPMAN'S DEATH MAKES HEADLINES AROUND THE WORLD.

CHAPMAN WAS 54. HIS GENIUS WAS FIRST REVEALED IN THE LATE 1950s...

MILLIONS OF PEOPLE INSPIRED BY THE LOTUS STORY WERE AFFECTED BY HIS DEATH.

HAZEL AND HER CHILDREN SHOW GREAT COURAGE IN THE FACE OF THIS TRAGIC LOSS.

THE FIRST THING COLIN WOULD HAVE WANTED IS FOR TEAM LOTUS TO CARRY ON.

I THINK SO, TOO!

DE ANGELIS AND SENNA WOULD CLOCK UP A FURTHER SEVEN WINS IN THE ENSUING YEARS, USING FIRST THE RENAULT AND LATER THE HONDA ENGINE.

THOUGH JABBY CROMBAC CONTINUES TO FOLLOW F1, HIS HEART ISN'T IN IT...

BUT TEAM LOTUS WOULD NEVER AGAIN BE WORLD CHAMPIONS FOLLOWING COLIN'S DEATH AND WOULD DISAPPEAR AT THE END OF THE 1994 SEASON.

IN 1992, COLIN AND HAZEL'S SON, CLIVE, FOUNDED 'CLASSIC TEAM LOTUS' TO RESTORE AND MAINTAIN LOTUS RACING CARS BUILT BY HIS FATHER. THEY CONTINUE TO DELIGHT PRESENT-DAY CROWDS BY RACING IN HISTORIC CAR RACES.

STARTING FROM NOTHING, COLIN CHAPMAN, THROUGH HIS INTELLIGENCE, PASSION AND BOUNDLESS ENERGY, DEMONSTRATED HIS ABILITY TO INSPIRE PEOPLE TO HELP HIM REALISE HIS DREAMS AND ENGINEER HIS MASTERPIECES. HE WILL FOREVER REMAIN THE INNOVATIVE GENIUS OF THE GOLDEN AGE OF FORMULA 1.

46